First World War
and Army of Occupation
War Diary
France, Belgium and Germany

58 DIVISION
175 Infantry Brigade
London Regiment
2/12 Battalion
1 February 1918 - 31 May 1919

WO95/3009/9-10

The Naval & Military Press Ltd
www.nmarchive.com
Published in association with The National Archives

Published by

The Naval & Military Press Ltd

Unit 10 Ridgewood Industrial Park,

Uckfield, East Sussex,

TN22 5QE England

Tel: +44 (0) 1825 749494

www.naval-military-press.com

www.nmarchive.com

This diary has been reprinted in facsimile from the original. Any imperfections are inevitably reproduced and the quality may fall short of modern type and cartographic standards.

Contents

Document type	Place/Title	Date From	Date To
Heading	WO95/3009/8 (Apr 1919 Missing)		
Heading	58 Division 175 Bde 1/12 London Regiment 1918 Feb-1919 May From 56 Div 168 Bde		
War Diary	Corbie	01/02/1918	06/02/1918
War Diary	Appilly	06/02/1918	06/02/1918
War Diary	Rouez	07/02/1918	07/02/1918
War Diary	Bois-De-Vieville	07/02/1918	21/02/1918
War Diary	Vendeuil	22/02/1918	25/02/1918
War Diary	Liez	25/02/1918	26/02/1918
War Diary	Tergnier Viry Noureuil	26/02/1918	27/02/1918
War Diary	Chauny	27/02/1918	28/02/1918
Miscellaneous	12 Battalion london Regt.	03/02/1918	03/02/1918
Miscellaneous	The Rangers Administrative Details 202	04/02/1918	04/02/1918
Miscellaneous	The Rangers	06/02/1918	06/02/1918
Miscellaneous	The Rangers Administrative Order No. 3	05/02/1918	05/02/1918
Operation(al) Order(s)	The Rangers Operation Order No. 100	05/02/1918	05/02/1918
Miscellaneous	Provisional Defence Scheme For Left Support Battalion, Vendeuil Subsector	15/02/1918	15/02/1918
Miscellaneous	Distribution		
Miscellaneous	Amendment to Operation Order No. 110	19/02/1918	19/02/1918
Operation(al) Order(s)	The Rangers Operation Order No. 110	19/02/1918	19/02/1918
Operation(al) Order(s)	The Rangers Operation Order No. 111	24/02/1918	24/02/1918
Miscellaneous	The Rangers Warning Order.	26/02/1918	26/02/1918
Miscellaneous	The Rangers	25/02/1916	25/02/1916
Miscellaneous	The Rangers Warning Order	26/02/1918	26/02/1918
Operation(al) Order(s)	The Rangers Operation Order No. 112	26/02/1918	26/02/1918
Operation(al) Order(s)	The Rangers Operation Order No. 113		
Heading	War Diary Rangers 12 London Regt. March 1918 Volume III		
War Diary	Le Epinois Sector	01/03/1918	26/03/1918
War Diary	Abbecourt Sector	27/03/1918	31/03/1918
Operation(al) Order(s)	The Rangers Operation Order No. 119	23/03/1918	23/03/1918
Operation(al) Order(s)	Operation Order No. 120	26/03/1918	26/03/1918
Miscellaneous	The Rangers 12th London Regt.		
Operation(al) Order(s)	The Rangers Operation Order No. 114	05/03/1918	05/03/1918
Miscellaneous	The rangers (Provisional Defence Scheme)		
Miscellaneous	Patrol Report For Night 7/8 March 1918	07/03/1918	07/03/1918
Miscellaneous	Patrol Report For Night 8.3.18	08/03/1918	08/03/1918
Diagram etc	Sketch Plan Shewing Route Taken By Patrol		
Miscellaneous	Patrol Report for Night 8/9 March 1918	08/03/1918	08/03/1918
Miscellaneous	Patrol Report for Night 10/11 Mar 1918	10/03/1918	10/03/1918
Miscellaneous	Patrol Report For Night 11/12 March 1918	11/03/1918	11/03/1918
Operation(al) Order(s)	The Rangers Operation Order No. 115	11/03/1918	11/03/1918
Operation(al) Order(s)	The Rangers Operation Order No. 116	13/03/1918	13/03/1918
Miscellaneous	Patrol Report for Night 13/4 March 1918	13/03/1918	13/03/1918
Miscellaneous	Patrol Report For Night 14/15 March 1918	14/03/1918	14/03/1918
Miscellaneous	Patrol Report For Night 15/18 March 1918	15/03/1918	15/03/1918
Map	Map		
Operation(al) Order(s)	The Rangers Operation Order No. 116	17/03/1918	17/03/1918
Operation(al) Order(s)	The Rangers Operation Order No. 117	17/03/1918	17/03/1918

Operation(al) Order(s)	The Rangers Operation Order No. 118	19/03/1918	19/03/1918
Heading	War Diary 12th Battn. The London Regiment. (The Rangers) April 1918		
Heading	War Diary Rangers 12 London Regt April 1918 Volume IV		
War Diary	Abbecourt Sector	01/04/1918	03/04/1918
War Diary	St Paul Aux Bois	03/04/1918	03/04/1918
War Diary	Andignicourt	03/04/1918	04/04/1918
War Diary	Laversine	04/04/1918	05/04/1918
War Diary	Villers-Cotterets	05/04/1918	05/04/1918
War Diary	Longeau	06/04/1918	06/04/1918
War Diary	Bois De Gentelles	07/04/1918	07/04/1918
War Diary	Villers-Bretonneux	07/04/1918	13/04/1918
War Diary	Blangy Wood	13/04/1918	15/04/1918
War Diary	Glisy	16/04/1918	18/04/1918
War Diary	Gentelles Wood	19/04/1918	30/04/1918
Miscellaneous	Appendices		
Operation(al) Order(s)	The Rangers Operation Order 121	02/04/1918	02/04/1918
Operation(al) Order(s)	The Rangers Operation Order 122	03/04/1918	03/04/1918
Operation(al) Order(s)	The Rangers Operation Order No. 123	04/04/1918	04/04/1918
Operation(al) Order(s)	The Rangers Operation Order No. 124	05/04/1918	05/04/1918
Operation(al) Order(s)	The Rangers Operation Order No. 125	07/03/1918	07/03/1918
Miscellaneous	Patrol Report		
Operation(al) Order(s)	The Rangers Operation Order No. 126	13/04/1918	13/04/1918
Operation(al) Order(s)	The Rangers Operation Order No. 127	15/04/1918	15/04/1918
Heading	War Diary The Rangers 12th London Regt. Volume V May 1918		
War Diary	Cachy	24/04/1918	27/04/1918
War Diary	Bussus Near Abbeville	27/04/1918	09/05/1918
War Diary	Warloy	10/05/1918	31/05/1918
Heading	The Rangers 12th London Regt War Diary From 1st June To 30 June 1918		
War Diary	C 20 B.5.5 Sheet 62d	01/06/1918	04/06/1918
War Diary	B 15.b.5.3.sheet 62d	05/06/1918	10/06/1918
War Diary	Pissy	10/06/1918	18/06/1918
War Diary	C 21.b. Sheet.62 HW	19/06/1918	30/06/1918
Heading	The Rangers 12 London Regt July 1st 1918 To July 31st 1918		
War Diary	In Line Senlis Sector	01/07/1918	25/07/1918
War Diary	Senlis Sector	27/07/1918	31/07/1918
Heading	175th Bde. 58th Div. 12th Battalion London Regiment (The Rangers)		
Heading	War Diary Aug 1st-31st 1918 The Rangers, 12 London Regt.		
War Diary	Trenches Senus Sector	31/07/1918	04/08/1918
War Diary	Vignacourt	05/08/1918	07/08/1918
War Diary	Bois Escardonneuse	07/08/1918	09/08/1918
War Diary	Front Line Nr Morlancourt	09/08/1918	13/08/1918
War Diary	Bois Escardonneuse	14/08/1918	21/08/1918
War Diary	J.12 (Sheet 620)	22/08/1918	22/08/1918
War Diary	Tailles Wood	22/08/1918	24/08/1918
War Diary	Happy Valley	25/08/1918	25/08/1918
War Diary	F.28c	26/08/1918	29/08/1918
War Diary	B.20	30/08/1918	31/08/1918
War Diary	Maricourt	01/09/1918	09/09/1918
War Diary	Epehy	10/09/1918	13/09/1918

War Diary	Bois Epinette	15/09/1918	17/09/1918
War Diary	Guyencourt	18/09/1918	24/09/1918
War Diary	Trones Wood	26/09/1918	28/09/1918
War Diary	Estree Cauchie	29/09/1918	30/09/1918
War Diary	Lievin Angres	01/10/1918	09/10/1918
War Diary	Nr Annay	09/10/1918	13/10/1918
War Diary	Fouquieres	13/10/1918	21/10/1918
War Diary	Cense De Choques (Sheet 44.)	22/10/1918	22/10/1918
War Diary	Rumegies	23/10/1918	26/10/1918
War Diary	Aix	27/10/1918	07/11/1918
War Diary	Quesnoy	08/11/1918	09/11/1918
War Diary	Peruwelz	09/11/1918	10/11/1918
War Diary	Neufmaison	10/11/1918	30/11/1918
War Diary	Stambruges	01/12/1918	21/12/1918
War Diary	Leuze	22/12/1918	31/12/1918
War Diary	Leuze Belgium	01/01/1919	22/02/1919
War Diary	Leuze	23/02/1919	31/03/1919
Heading	April 1919 Missing		
War Diary	Leuze	01/05/1919	31/05/1919
Heading	WO95/3009/9/10		
Heading	58 Division 175 Bde 2/12 London Regt 1915 Sept-1916 Feb 1917 Jan 1918 Jan Absorbed By 1/12 Bn 1918 Feb		

WO 95

3009/8

(Apr 1919 missing)

58 DIVISION

175 BDE

1/12 London Regiment

1918 FEB — 1919 MAY

FROM 56 DIV 168 BD
+
ABSORBED 2/12 BN 1918 FEB

Instructions regarding War Diaries and Intelligence Summaries are contained in F. S. Regs., Part II. and the Staff Manual respectively. Title pages will be prepared in manuscript.

WAR DIARY
or
INTELLIGENCE SUMMARY.
(Erase heading not required.)

Army Form C. 2118.

12 London Rgt

Vol 14

Place	Date	Hour	Summary of Events and Information	Remarks and references to Appendices
CORBIE	1st to 4th	2/18	Training under Company arrangements	
CORBIE	5-2-18		Lieut Colonel A.D BAYLIFFE C.M.G returned from leave & assumed command of the Battalion.	
	6-2-18	12 noon	Battalion entrained for new area	OO 109 + appendices att.
APPILLY		6.30pm	Battalion arrived and detrained	
		8 pm	Battalion embussed.	
ROUEZ	7-2-18	4.30am	Battalion less "D" Coy arrived in billets	
		6.30am	"D" Coy arrived at FORT LIEZ and relieved one Company 18th LIVERPOOL REGT	
			Battalion rested	
		4 pm	Battalion moved by march route to BOIS DE VIEVILLE	
BOIS-DE-VIEVILLE		7 pm	Battalion arrived in Camp	
	8-2-18		Battalion employed on Camp fatigues	
	9-2-18		- ditto - and working parties on VENDEUIL SWITCH	
	10-2-18		- ditto - - ditto - - ditto - Divisional Commander visited Sites selected for defensive positions to be held by one company in Battle Area	
	11-2-18		Battalion employed on Camp fatigues and working parties as yesterday. Inspection of Battalion by Commanding Officer.	
	12-2-18		Battalion employed on Camp fatigues & working parties on VENDEUIL SWITCH.	
	13-2-18	10 am	Ditto - Ditto - and Company training. Commanding Officer attended Brigade Conference and subsequently visited VENDEUIL SWITCH with G.O.C and discussed system of defence. - A draft of 13 casuals arrived today.	
	14-2-18	10 am	Company training and Camp fatigues - Working parties on VENDEUIL SWITCH. Company Commanders conference and visited VENDEUIL SWITCH to study ground & arrange dispositions for defence.	
	15-2-18	10 am to 4.30pm	"A" Company commenced digging selected position in Battle zone. Remaining Companies employed in training and Camp fatigues. A draft of 8 casuals arrived from Depot Bn today -	

D. D. & L., London, E.C.
(A8004) Wt. W1771/M2-31 750,000 5/17 Sch. 52 Forms/C2118/14

Army Form C. 2118.

Instructions regarding War Diaries and Intelligence Summaries are contained in F. S. Regs., Part II. and the Staff Manual respectively. Title pages will be prepared in manuscript.

WAR DIARY
or
INTELLIGENCE SUMMARY.

(*Erase heading not required.*)

Place	Date	Hour	Summary of Events and Information	Remarks and references to Appendices
BOIS DE VIEVILLE	16-2-18	10 am to 4.30 pm	"A" Company continued work on the Battle zone assisted by "D" Company "B" Company employed wiring VENDEUIL SWITCH "C" Company on duty –	
	17-2-18	10 am to 4.30 pm	"A" Company continued work on Battle zone assisted by "C" Company. "B" Company wiring VENDEUIL SWITCH "D" Company on duty and found 1 platoon to prepared wiring material at LIEZ DUMP During the day enemy shelled slightly the South end of REMIGNY and new work upon RONQUENET FARM by 4.2 hows. at extreme range. Enemy aircraft very active all day.	
		4.15 pm	Enemy aircraft attacked our O.B near FRIERES FAILLOUEL and brought it down in flames	
		6.40 pm	Enemy 'planes crossed our lines and 3 minutes later directing signals – strings of 4 white lights were seen to go up NE of FORT VENDEUIL The lights continued at 1½ minute intervals until 8.30pm when all enemy 'planes returned home – On the outward journey the 'planes travelled towards LIEZ & TERGNIER.	
	18-2-18	8.30 am	"C" Company, two platoons repairing LIEZ – VENDEUIL FORT ROAD 1 platoon preparing wiring material at LIEZ DUMP	
	~~[illegible]~~	10 am to 4.30 pm	"A" + "D" Companies working on Battle zone "B" Company wiring VENDEUIL SWITCH	
	19-2-18	8.30 am	"B" Company, two platoons repair LIEZ – VENDEUIL FORT ROAD	
		10 am to 3.30 pm	"A" + "D" Companies and 30 or H.Q. Company working on Battle zone. "C" Company wiring VENDEUIL SWITCH	
	20-2-18	10 am to 3.30 pm	"B" + "D" Companies on Battle zone "C" Company wiring VENDEUIL SWITCH "A" Company on Camp fatigues.	
	21-2-18		"B" + "D" Companies on Battle zone "C" Company wiring VENDEUIL SWITCH	

D. D. & L., London, E.C.
(A8004) Wt. W1771/M2731 750,000 5/17 Sch. 52 Forms/C2118/14

Instructions regarding War Diaries and Intelligence Summaries are contained in F. S. Regs., Part II. and the Staff Manual respectively. Title pages will be prepared in manuscript.

WAR DIARY
or
INTELLIGENCE SUMMARY.
(Erase heading not required.)

Army Form C. 2118.

Place	Date	Hour	Summary of Events and Information	Remarks and references to Appendices
VENDEUIL	22-2-18		"A"+"C" Coys on Battle zone	
			"D" Coy. wiring VENDEUIL SWITCH	
		6 pm	Battalion relieved 10th London Regt in VENDEUIL SECTOR	OO 110 + amendment attached
	~~23-2-18~~	10.30 pm	Relief complete.	
	23-2-18		Trench routine + working parties	
	24-2-18		Trench routine + working parties.	
	25-2-18		Trench routine + working parties	
		6 pm	Battalion relieved by 7th QUEENS' REGT	OO 111 att.
		10.10 pm	Relief complete -	
LIEZ		10 pm	"A" Coy arrived FORT LIEZ, Bn HQ arrived LIEZ VILLAGE	
		11.30 pm	"B" Coy arrived FORT LIEZ, "C+D" Coys arrived LIEZ VILLAGE	
	26-2-18		Battalion moved by March route to VIRY NOUREUIL & TERGNIER	Administrative details attached Warning Order attached.
TERGNIER VIRY NOUREUIL		4 pm	A+B Coys arrived in Billets	
		5 pm	"C" + "D" Coys and Battn HQ arrived in Billets	
	27-2-18		Battalion moved by march route to CHAUGNY	OO 112 att.
CHAUNY		pm	Battalion arrived in Billets	
			C.O + Company Commanders visited the line L'EPINOIS SECTOR	
	28-2-18	5.30 p	Battalion moved to relieve 6th LONDON REGT in L'HERMITAGE SECTION	OO 113 att.
		10 pm	Relief complete.	
		2.30 pm	Received order by wire "Take Precautionary Action" - Notified Coys with instructions.	
		5.30	Received instructions to carry out relief of 6th LONDON REGT.	

A. G. Baylif[?]
Lieut Colonel
Comdg "The Rangers" 12th London Regt

D. D. & L., London, E.C.
(A8004) Wt. W1771/M2931 750,000 5/17 Sch. 52 Forms/C2118/14

12 BATTALION
No. [illegible]
Date [illegible]
LONDON REGT.

11

[illegible]

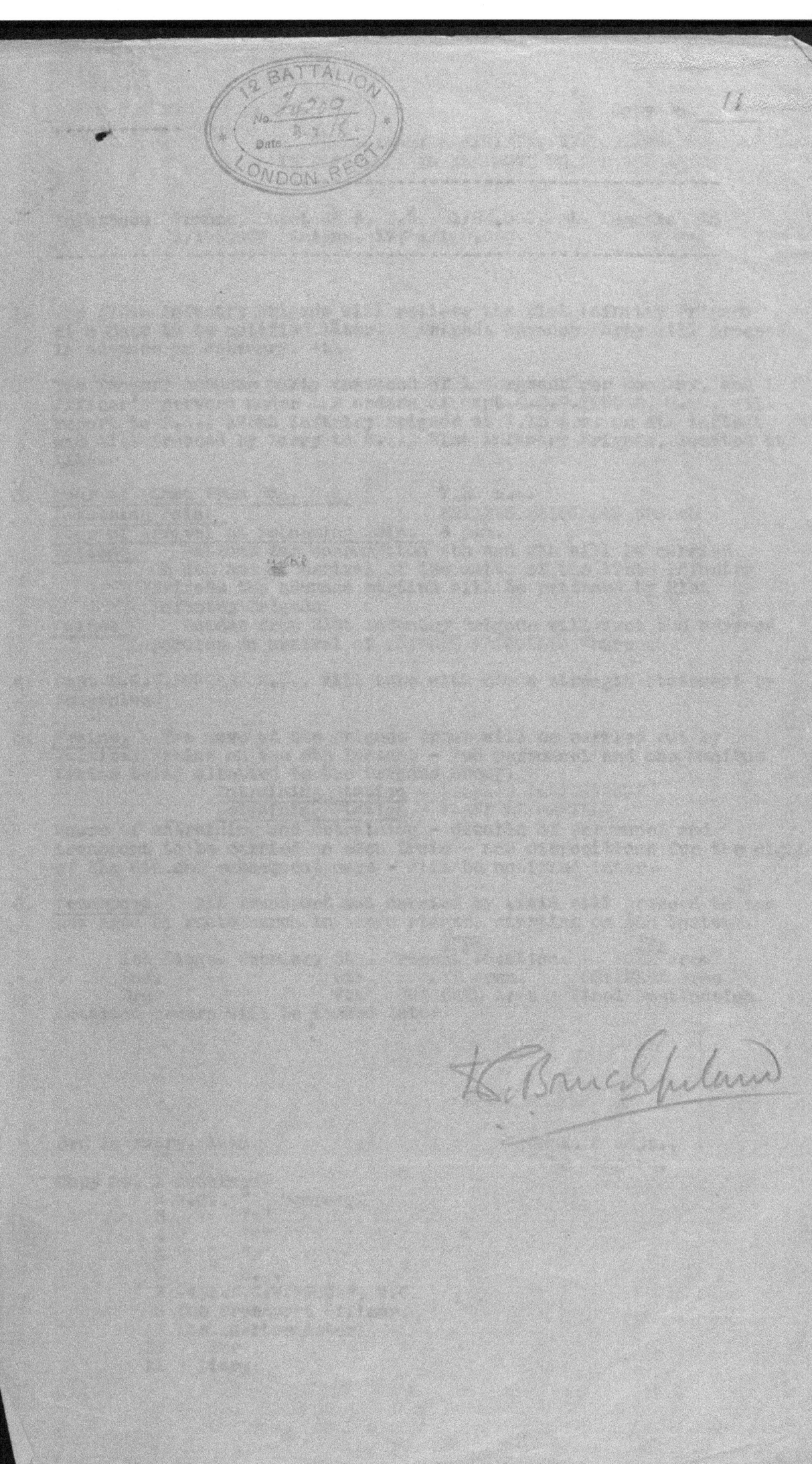

SECRET. "The Rangers." Copy No. 13

ADMINISTRATIVE ORDERS (No2)

in connection with

[illegible]

1. [illegible]
Brigade Entraining Officer:- Capt. [illegible]
Battalion Entraining Officer:- Capt. [illegible]
The Battalion (less Transport and loading party) will travel by the 2nd personnel train on the 9th instant.
Bicycles will be carried in the covered wagon allotted to this train.
Transport and loading party as under will travel by omnibus train on 9th instant:-
Loading Party. 1 Officer, 1 N.C.O. and 15 men, (to be detailed by "A" Company.
Officer i/c omnibus Train Transport. 2/Lt. [illegible]

17 Transport personnel.
8 Limbers and horses.
1 Water Cart and horses.
1 Mess Cart and horse.
1 Maltese Cart and horse.
1 Signal Limber and horses
4 Riders (C.O., 2 i/c, Adjt., [illegible])

All ranks travelling by train will carry one blanket a man.
On arrival at the detraining station ([illegible]) the Battalion will probably proceed to its destination in [illegible]
The Quartermaster will arrange to [illegible] rations, fuel and rations for 9th instant with personnel trains.

2. Baggage.
All Stores and baggage will be conveyed to the entraining station [illegible], by lorry, and loaded on the omnibus train, 2 lorries being allotted to the Battalion for this purpose.

3. [illegible]
The Transport Officer will arrange to carry to the entraining station all [illegible] and twenty filled [illegible] per gun. These will be unloaded at the station and carried by Companies on the personnel train.

4. Transport by Road.
All Transport not detailed to travel by train will travel by road, starting on 8th instant under the orders of [illegible]
The Transport Officer will travel with this column.
The Transport Officer will detail one mounted N.C.O. to report to the [illegible] at Brigade H.Q. at 7 a.m., 8th instant for billeting party.

5. Marching out State.
Marching out state issued herewith to those concerned.

[signature]
Capt. & Adjt.,
The Rangers.

Issued at 11.30 AM.
4th February, 191[illegible]

Copy No. 1 Retained.
2 O.C. "A" Company.
3 "B"
4 "C"
5 "D"
6 H.Q.
7 The Transport Officer.

No. 8 The Quartermaster.
9 Capt. [illegible]
10 Capt. [illegible]
11 2/Lt. [illegible]
12 [illegible]
13) War
14) Diary.

"The Rangers."

	Off.	O.R.	Animals.	2-wheeled vehicles.	4-wheeled horsed vehicles.	Bicycles.
Travelling with Adv. Party by lorry on 4/2/1918.	1	6	-	-	-	-
Travelling with Transport Column by road on 5/2/1918.	1	[illegible]	[illegible]	1	6	-
Travelling by 1st Personnel train on 6/2/1918	-	-	-	-	-	-
Travelling by 2nd. Personnel train on 6/2/1918.	27	751	-	-	-	5
Travelling by Vehicle train on 6/2/1918.	1	21	[illegible]	3	8	-
Total Marching Out Strength of Unit.	30	[illegible]	[illegible]	4	14	5

[signature]

Capt. & Adjt.,
The Rangers.

4th February, 1918.

SECRET. [illegible] Copy No. 14

ADMINISTRATIVE INSTRUCTIONS No. 3.

1. Trains.
Previous instructions regarding entraining and detraining stations are cancelled.
The [illegible] Infantry Brigade Group will entrain at [illegible] and detrain at [illegible].
The times of departure and arrival of trains will be notified later.

2. Billets.
(a) Parties for conveyance of stores and blankets to [illegible] station will report at [illegible] Brigade H.Q., at 6.0 a.m., 4th instant.
The Quartermaster will detail two guides to take over billets at this time.
(b) On the arrival of the Battalion at its destination the Quartermaster will arrange as soon as the billets to collect blankets, etc., from the [illegible] train.

3. Rations.
The Transport personnel travelling on the earlier train will probably bivouac somewhere for the night of the 5th instant.
The Quartermaster will arrange that rations for the Transport personnel and the forage for the 7th instant, are therefore carried separately.

Issued at 2100

5th January, 1918.

[signature]

Capt. & Adjt.,
[illegible]

Copy No. 1 Retained.
2 O.C., "A" Company.
3 "B"
4 "C"
5 "D"
6 H.Q.
7 The Transport Officer.
8 The Quartermaster.
9 Capt. [illegible]
10 Capt. [illegible]
11 Lieut. [illegible]
12 [illegible]
13 War
14 Diary.

SECRET.

Ref. Maps AMIENS, 1/100,000,
St. QUENTIN, 1/100,000 and
Sheet 66c, 1/40,000.

"The Rangers."

Copy No. 14

OPERATION ORDERS No.109.

1. The 175th Infantry Brigade will move from its present area to-morrow 6th instant in connection with the relief of the 21st Infantry Brigade.

2. The Rangers will relieve the 18th Liverpool Regiment to-morrow 6th instant, moving by rail and road, entraining at CORBIE Station and detraining at APILLY, thence by bus to Camp ROUEZ.

3. The move will be carried out as under:-
   (a) Transport and loading party as detailed in Administrative Details, No. 2, dated 4th February, will travel by the omnibus train departing at 9 a.m., and arriving at4 p.m. These details will arrive at CORBIE Station at 6.30 a.m.
   (b) The Battalion (less Transport) will move by the 2nd Personnel train starting at 12 noon and arriving at 7 p.m. The Battalion will arrive at CORBIE Station at 11 a.m., marching there by Companies at 100 yards interval in the following order: Band, H.Q., "A", "B", "C", "D", the head of column to pass road junction 200 yards South of the Church at 10.45 a.m.

4. All blankets (less one per man to be carried) in tight bundles of 10 and all baggage will be dumped at the Quartermaster's Stores by 5.30 a.m.

5. Dress: Greatcoats will be worn and one blanket carried in pack.

Issued at ________

5th February, 1918.

Capt. & Adjt.,
"The Rangers."

Copy No. 1 Retained.
2 O.C., "A" Company.
3 "B"
4 "C"
5 "D"
6 H.Q.
7 The Transport Officer.
8 The Quartermaster.
9 Capt. F.H.BAKER.
10 Capt. A.J.REINCKE.
11 2/Lt. H.V.ROLLINS.
12 R.S.M.
13) War
14) Diary.

"The Rangers." Copy No. 11

PROVISIONAL DEFENCE SCHEME
FOR LEFT SUPPORT BATTALION, VENDEUIL
SUBSECTOR.

1. The Battalion of the 175th Infantry Brigade in the Forward Zone will be known as the Outpost Battalion, the Battalion located in FORT LIEZ and LIEZ will be known as the right Support Battalion, the Battalion located in the BOIS DE VIEVILLE will be known as the Left Support Battalion.

2. The limits of the forward zone are coloured red, the limits of the Battle Zone are coloured blue on the map posted in Battalion Orderly Room.

3. While an attack on a large scale is most probable from the N.E., i.e. with the left of the attack on the OISE Valley, the possibility of an attack in conjunction with it from the East or from the S.E. by ST. FIRMIN must not be lost sight of.

On the other hand an attack from the East or S.E. unaccompanied by an attack from the N.E. is improbable, as the difficulties in getting guns across the OISE Valley would prevent the enemy from being able to follow up his initial success.

It would therefore appear that the most probable form of attack we shall have to face from the East or S.E. is a subsidiary attack whose objective would be to break through our line, with a view to seizing the crossings over the CROZAT CANAL at LIEZ and JUSSY and by coming in on the flank to help the main attack.

Although such an attack would be a small affair compared with the large attack from the N.E., still it would be delivered by a force of at least two Divisions and therefore would be a large attack compared with our rather extended line.

An attack from the East or S.E. will fall directly on our Outpost Battalion, and, in the event of the attack breaking through the Outpost Zone, on our part of the Battle Zone - 3000 yards in rear of the Outpost Zone.

Before the main attack from the N.E. can directly effect the 175th Infantry Brigade it will have

(a) To break through the Outpost Zone of the Division on our left.
(b) To advance across the front of the Battle Zone of the Division on our left.
(c) To advance at least 4000 yards.
(d) To cross the heights MOY - CERIZY (H.23.) - LAMBAY FARM (H.10).

To meet the possibility of this attack breaking through the defences of the Division on our left, the VENDEUIL - LY FONTAINE switch, which consists of three lines of trenches on the reverse slope, with good observation from just over the crest and with its right firmly pivoted on FORT VENDEUIL and its left on LY FONTAINE has been constructed. This switch is considered as part of the Battle Zone.

To meet either or both of these attacks the following dispositions will be taken up at once by the left Support Battalion on the order from the Brigade "Man Battle Zone." In the event of the S.O.S. Signal going up on our front or of intense bombardment suddenly opening on our front or on the Brigades on our flanks Companies will at once assemble on their alarm posts but will not move without orders from Battalion H.Q.

on receipt of orders

Left Support Battalion.

"B" and "C" Companies will on receipt of orders man the FORT VENDEUIL - LY FONTAINE switch between FORT VENDEUIL (exclusive) and hill 90 (H.10.d.) inclusive. This position is allotted to Companies as follows:- "B" Company FORT VENDEUIL (exclusive) to CISTERNE WOOD (inclusive): "C" Company CISTERNE WOOD (exclusive) to Hill 90, (inclusive).
"A" Company will man that part of the Battle Zone between the valley North of RONQUENET FARM (inclusive) and the Brigade Northern Boundary.
One Company in reserve will move to the bank at N.23.a.9.9. This Reserve Company will not be moved thence without orders from Bn. H.Q.

L. G. Buckland [signature]
CAPT. & ADJT.
"THE RANGERS" 12th LONDON REGIMENT.

15th February, 1918.

DISTRIBUTION:

Copy No. 1 & 2 Retained.
3 O.C., "A" Company.
4 "B"
5 "C"
6 "D"
7 H.Q.
8 The Transport Officer.
9 The Quartermaster.
10. R.S.M.
11.) War
12.) Diary.

"THE RANGERS" ORDERLY ROOM No. OO 110/1 Date 19-2-16 LONDON REGT.

TO ALL RECIPIENTS OF OPERATION ORDER 110.

AMENDMENT TO OPERATION ORDER No.110.

Please delete ~~pa~~ first paragraph in para. 6, and substitute the following:-

6. The Transport Officer will arrange that Lewis Gun limbers remain with their Companies on the night 21/22nd February so that Lewis Guns and ammunition can move at dusk.

[signature]

Capt. & Adjt.,
"The Rangers."

19th February, 1917.

SECRET.   "The Rangers."   Copy No. [illegible]

OPERATION ORDER No. 110.

Reference Sheet 66c, S.W., 1/20,000.

1. "The Rangers" will relieve the 2/10th Lonion Regiment in the Outpost Line, VENDEUIL Sub-Section on the night 22/23rd February, 1918, as under:-
"B" Coy, Rangers will relieve "D" Coy, 2/10th L.R. as Rt. Front Coy.
"C" " " " " "A" " " " " Centre Company.
"D" " " " " "C" " " " " Lt. Front Coy.
"A" " " " " "B" " " " " Support Company.

2. Companies will move in the above order by platoons at 100 yards interval, the leading platoon to reach fork roads at N.17.d.7.3. at 6 p.m., where guides will meet the Battalion.

3. Reconnaissance of the line will be carried out as under:-
Company Commanders and the Pioneer Officer will visit the line on the morning of the 20th instant.
Platoon Commanders holding forward Posts and the Intelligence Officer with the Scout Section will proceed to the line on the 21st instant, reporting to Battalion H.Q. in FORT VENDEUIL at 3 p.m. This party will stay with the 2/10th London Regiment until relief is complete. One day's rations will be carried by this party.
The Transport Officer will arrange with the Transport Officer of the 2/10th London Regiment to send a sufficient number of Transport personnel to proceed with the 2/10th London Regiment Transport to the line on the nights of 20th and 21st in order to reconnoitre tracks and forward ration dumps.

4. An advance party of 2 Signallers per Company and 4 per Battalion H.Q., the R.S.M. and C.S.Ms will proceed to the line to take over trench stores, signal stations, etc., reporting to Battalion H.Q. in FORT VENDEUIL at 10.30 a.m., 22nd instant.
This party will parade at Orderly Room at 9.15 a.m., 22nd instant.

5. Blankets at the rate of 1 per man will be taken into the line. The surplus blanket will be returned to the Quartermaster's Stores.
All blankets in tight bundles of 10 and other baggage will be dumped at Battalion H.Q. by 3 p.m., 22nd instant.
All baggage will be clearly marked with name of Company and showing whether for the line or stores.

6. The Transport Officer will arrange that Lewis Gun limbers report to their Companies so that Lewis Guns and ammunition can move with the leading platoon of Companies.
All other baggage will be moved as arranged between the Transport Officer and the Quartermaster. 2 G.S. wagons are available, and will stay at the Transport lines after delivery of rations on the 22nd instant.

7. On relief the 2/10th London Regiment will become Left Support Battalion and be accommodated in BOIS DE VIEVILLE, taking over all dispositions and orders as regards manning the Battle Zone and VENDEUIL - LY FONTAINE Switch from "The Rangers" which will be re-c-nnoitred by Officers of the 2/10th Lonion Regiment on the 20th inst.

8. The Works Officers will arrange to hand over details of all work in progress. He will also arrange that the continuity of work taken over from the 2/10th Lonion Regiment is not interfered with by the relief.

9. An advance party of the 2/10th London Regiment will be expected on the morning of the 22nd instant.

10. Receipted lists of all stores handed over to and taken over from the 2/10th London Regiment will be handed into Orderly Room immediately after relief.

11. Completion of relief will be notified to Battalion H.Q. by wiring the Company Commander's surname only.

12. Battalion H.Q. will close at Camp de VIEVILLE at 5.30 p.m. and will re-open in FORT de VERDEUIL on arrival.

K.G.B. McAlpine

Issued at 6 pm

Capt. & Adjt.,
"The Rangers."

19th February, 1918.

Copy No. 1 Retained.
2 175th Infantry Brigade.
3 2/10th London Regiment.
4 O.C., "A" Company.
5 "B"
6 "C"
7 "D"
8 H.Q.
9 The Works Officer.
10 The Medical Officer.
11 The Transport Officer.
12 The Pioneer Officer.
13 The Quartermaster.
14 R.S.M.
15) War
16) Diary.

Transport lines do not move

KGBC

SECRET. "The Rangers." Copy No. 15

OPERATION ORDER No.111.

Reference sheet 66c, S.W., 1/20,000.

1\. The Rangers will be relieved on the night of the 25/26th February by the 7th Battalion, the Queen's Regiment, and will go into the Right Support.
Order of relief as under:-
"B" Company, 7th Queen's will relieve "B" Company, Rangers.
"D" " " " " " "C" " "
"A" " " " " " "D" " "
"C" " " " " " "A" " "

2\. When relieved Companies will move as under by platoons at not less than 50 yards interval:-
"B" Company to FORT LIEZ, via cross roads U.1.a.25.20.
"A" Company to FORT LIEZ, via fork roads N.17.d.75.25.
"C" Company to LIEZ, via cross roads N.24.d.95.75.
"D" Company to LIEZ, via cross roads N.24.d.95.75.

3\. One guide per platoon and one per Company H.Q. to report at Battalion H.Q. at 3.30 p.m. to meet relieving troops.

4\. Advance Parties. "A" Company under arrangements to be made by O.C. Company. "B" Company 1 N.C.O. and 1 signaller to report to Lt. K.H.J. ANDERSON at FORT LIEZ at 3 p.m. "C" and "D" Companies 1 N.C.O. and 1 signaller per Company to report to the Quartermaster in LIEZ village at 3 p.m. These parties will take over stores, signal stations, etc. from 7th Queens.

5\. Blankets and baggage will be dumped as under by 7 p.m.:-

H.Q. and "A" Company.	-	Outside W. entrance of FORT VENDEUIL. (About N.18.c.1.5.)
"B", "C" and "D" Coys.	-	Company Ration Dumps.
Pioneer Platoon & Aid Post.	-	Fork Roads, O.13.c.10.10.

6\. Lewis Gun limbers will report as in para. 5, and will follow the last platoon of their respective Companies. They will remain with Companies for the night 25/26th February.

7\. Water carts will be taken one to Battalion H.Q. and one to FORT LIEZ, where they will remain for the night.

8\. On arrival at Right Support Position Defence Scheme Dispositions will be handed over to O.C. Companies by Officers of the 9th London Regiment remaining behind for that purpose. Companies will take over from corresponding Companies of 7th Queen's.

9\. Completion of relief in Outpost Line will be notified to Battalion H.Q. by wiring the Company Commander's surname. O.C. Companies will not leave their headquarters in the Outpost Line until their message reporting the relief complete has been acknowledged. Completion of relief at Right Support position will be notified by wiring Company Commanders' initials to new Battalion H.Q.

10\. On completion of relief of Outpost Line Battalion H.Q. move to QUARRY at N.31.b.8.3.

HEClarke
Lieut. & A/Adjt.
"The Rangers."

Issued at 11 p.m.

24th February, 1918.

DISTRIBUTION.

Copy No. 1 Retained.
2 175th Infantry Brigade.
3 7th Bn. The Queen's Regt.
4 Major W.G. Worthington, M.C.
5 Capt. K.H.J. Anderson.
6 O.C., "A" Company.
7 "B"
8 "C"
9 "D"
10 H.Q.
11 The Transport Officer.
12 The Quartermaster.
13 The Medical Officer.
14 R.S.M.
15) War
16) Diary.

SECRET. "The Rangers." Copy No. 12

WARNING ORDER.

26th February, 1918.
"The Rangers" will be relieved at Right Support position by 7th Battalion, The Buffs, and will proceed by ~~tmmm~~ route march as under:-
"C", "D" and Headquarters to VIRY NOREUIL.
"A" and "B" Companies to TERGNIER.
"C" and "D" Companies will be relieved about 12 noon; "A" and "B" Companies about 2 p.m.
Transport (less Lewis Gun limbers, field cookers, water carts, which will accompany the Companies) will proceed to CHAUNY SUD.

27th February, 1918.
The Battalion will march from VIRY NOREUIL and TERGNIER to CHAUNY SUD.

28th February, 1918.
Battalion Headquarters and two Companies will relieve left of ~~th~~ sixth London Regiment in the line. Two Companies remain at CHAUNY SUD.

Further particulars and instructions will be issued later.

H.C. Clarke

Lieut. & A/Adjt.,
"The Rangers."

Issued at 11 p.m.

24th February, 1918.

Copy No. 1 Retained.
2 Major W.G.Worthington, M.C.
3 O.C., "A" Company.
4 "B"
5 "C"
6 "D"
7 H.Q.
8 The Transport Officer.
9 The Quartermaster.
10 The Medical Officer.
11 R.S.M.
12) War
13) Diary.

SECRET. "The Rangers." Copy No. 15

ADMINISTRATIVE DETAILS IN CONNECTION WITH MOVE TO VIRY NOREUIL AND TERGNIER.

Reference: WARNING ORDER dated 25th February, 1918.
Sheet 66c S.W., 1/20,000, and Sheet 70d N.W., 1/20,000.

1. When relieved Companies will move by platoons at 50 yards interval with a minimum of 10 minutes between Companies.

2. The Quartermaster's Stores will be dumped by 10 a.m. at B.8.b.20.70. where 2 lorries will report at that hour to convey stores to CHAUGNY SUD.

3. Blankets, valises, etc., will be dumped as under by 12 noon. H.Q. at QUARRY, "C" and "D" Companies at N.32.c.5.3. and "A" and "B" Companies at LIEZ FORT. Guards, who will also act as loading parties, will be left over these dumps. 2 lorries will be available to move the baggage reporting at Brigade H.Q. at 6 p.m. O.C., "A" Company will detail an Officer to be in charge of the Guard. He will report to the Adjutant at 10 a.m. for instructions.

4. Lewis Gun limbers will move with their respective Companies and remain with them for night 26/27th February.

5. Field cookers are at present parked in LIEZ village and will move with their Companies. O.C., Companies will arrange to collect their cookers where necessary. "C" and "D" Companies cookers will be ready to move at 12 noon. "A" and "B" Companies at 2 p.m.

6. The water cart at the QUARRY will move in rear of H.Q.Company and will remain in VIRY NOREUIL for the night. Water cart at LIEZ FORT will move in rear of "A" and "B" Companies and will remain in TERGNIER for the night.
Maltese Cart and Mess Cart will follow in rear of H.Q.Company and will remain at VIRY NOREUIL.

7. Advance Party. C.Q.M.Ss, Sergt. REEVES and Sergt BOND will report at Battalion H.Q. at 10 a.m. and will proceed on bicycles to the new billets.

8. Rations for the 27th will be delivered at new billets to-morrow.

9. Transport (less Officers' charges and vehicles mentioned above) will move direct to CHAUGNY SUD, clearing the Transport lines at BOIS HALLOT by 1 p.m.

10. On completion of relief Battalion H.Q. will move to VIRY NOREUIL.

H Clarke
Lieut. & A/Adjt.,
"The Rangers."

Issued at 11.45 p.m.

25th February, 1918.

DISTRIBUTION.

Copy No. 1 Retained.
2 175th Infantry Brigade.
3 The Buffs.
4 O.C., "A" Company.
5 "B"
6 "C"
7 "D"
8 H.Q.
9 The Transport Officer.
10 The Quartermaster.
11 The Medical Officer.
12 R.S.M.
13 Sergt. REEVES.
14 Sergt. T.J.BUNN.
15) War
16) Diary.

SECRET.

"The Rangers."

Copy No. 13

WARNING ORDER.

Reference Sheet 70d, N.E., 1/20,000.

1 "The Rangers Headquarters and "C" and "D" Companies will relieve the left of the 8th Londons in the line on 28th February, 1918. "A" and "B" Companies will remain at CHAUGNY SUD.

2 Reconnaissance. O.C., "C" and "D" Companies will reconnoitre the position on the 27th February, and will report at 8th Bn. Headquarters LA FORTELLE (H.9.b.) at 11 a.m. They will report at Bn. Headquarters at 9 a.m. where a lorry will be ready to ~~xx~~ take them up.

3 All work in hand will be taken over so that there may be continuity of policy.

4. Defence Schemes or instructions, maps, aeroplane photographs, etc., relating to the new sector will be taken over. on relief –

Issued at 2 pm

26th February, 1918.

Lieut. & A/Adjt.,
"The Rangers."

SECRET. "The Rangers." Copy No. 13

OPERATION ORDER No.112.

Reference Sheet 70d, N.W., 1/20,000.

1. The Battalion will march from present locations to billets at CHAUGNY SUD. H.Q., "C" and "D" Companies, in that order, will pass road junction at A.15.d.9.7. at 5.30 p.m. "A" and "B" Companies, in that order, will pass road junction at T.25.d.3.5. at 5.30 p.m.
Route: VIRY NOUREUIL - CHAUGNY.
All movements will be with 50 yards interval between platoons and 10 minutes between Companies.

2. Lewis Gun limbers and field cookers will move with their respective Companies. One water cart will move with "A" and "B" Companies, the second water cart and the Maltese Cart with H.Q.

3. Blankets, valises, etc., of H.Q., "C" and "D" Companies will be dumped at Battalion H.Q. before the Companies move off; of "A" and "B" Companies at a point in TERGNIER to be agreed between O.C., "A" and "B" Companies before the Companies move off. Location to be notified to Battalion H.Q. as early as possible to-morrow morning. Loading parties as to-day. O.C., Companies concerned will arrange to leave an officer at TERGNIER. O.C. "C" Company will detail an officer for VIRY NOUREUIL.
Lorries will report at 6 p.m.

4. Advance Party. C.Q.M.S.s of "C" and "D" Companies and Sergt. REEVE (mounted on bicycles) will report to Lieut. A.J.REINCKE at Battalion H.Q. at 9 a.m.
C.Q.M.S.s of "A" and "B" Companies will report to Lieut. REINCKE at the Quartermaster's Stores, MIRROR MANUFACTORY, CHAUGNY SUD (A.3.c.) at 2 p.m.

5. Battalion H.Q. will close at VIRY NOUREUIL at 5 p.m. and open at CHAUGNY SUD on arrival.

H.E.Blake

Issued at 10.30.p.m.
26th February, 1918.

Lieut. & A/Adjt.,
The Rangers.

Copy No. 1 Retained.
2 O.C., "A" Company.
3 "B"
4 "C"
5 "D"
6 H.Q.
7 The Transport Officer.
8 The Quartermaster.
9 The Medical Officer.
10 Lieut. A.J.REINCKE.
11 R.S.M.
12 Sergt. REEVE.
13 } War
14 } Diary.
15 173rd Infantry Brigade.
16 175th Infantry Brigade.

Copy No..15....

"THE RANGERS".

OPERATION ORDER No. 113

Ref. Sheet 70D N.W. 1/20000.

1. The Rangers Hd.Qrs. & "C" & "D" Coys. will relieve the 6th. Londons in the line to-night 28th. Feb./1st. March.
   "C" Coy. Rangers will relieve "C" Coy. 6th. Londons.
   "D" " " " " "A" " " "
   Details of take over as arranged between Coy. Comdrs.

   "A" & "B" Coys. will remain at CHAUNY SUD under command of Capt. V.L.Burnside.

2. Relieving Coys. will move by Platoons at 5 minutes interval between Platoons, 10 minutes between Coys., in order "D", "C", Hd.Qrs. The head of the column will cross the CANAL at G.9.a.15.75 at 5.30 pm Route :- LE BOSQUET - SINCENY - LES HUTTES DE ROUY cross roads H.3.c.7.7.

3. Guides - 1 per platoon, 1 per Coy. Hd.Qrs. and 1 for Hd.Qrs. - will be at cross roads H.3.c.7.7. Guides for each post will be at their platoon Hd.Qrs.

4. Lewis Gun limbers and Field Cookers will move with their respective Coys. The former will return to Transport lines after delivering L.G.s etc. at Coy. Hd.Qrs.

5. Blankets and baggage will be dumped opposite Qr.Mr. Stores by 4 p.m. and will be loaded before Coys. parade. Any surplus kit to be at the Qr.Mr.Stores by the same hour.

6. One water cart will move with the baggage vehicles and will remain at new Bn. Hd.Qrs. The other water cart will remain with "A" & "B" Coys. Maltese cart will proceed with the baggage vehicles and will return after delivering stores at the Aid Post.

7. The R.S.M., Sgt. Griffiths and 5 Signallers from Hd. Qrs., C.S.M.s and 1 Signaller per Coy. from "C" & "D" Coys. will report at Qr.Mr. Stores at 11 a.m. and will proceed to the line for the purpose of taking over trench stores, signal stations etc.

8. Completion of relief will be notified to Bn. Hd.Qrs. by wiring Coy. Comdrs. initials.

9. Bn. Hd.Qrs. will close at CHAUNY SUD at 5 p.m. and open at LA FORTELLE on arrival.

10. ACKNOWLEDGE.

(Sgd.) H.E.Clarke, Lieut.
A/Adjt. "The Rangers".

(over.)

Issued at ....

Copy No.	1	Retained.
	2	175th. Inf. Bde.
	3.	174th. Inf. Bde.
	4.	8th. London Regt.
	5.	Maj. W.C.Worthington.
	6.	O.C. "A" Coy.
	7.	" "B" "
	8.	" "C" "
	9.	" "D" "
	10.	" Hd.Qrs.
	11.	The Transport Officer.
	12	The Quartermaster.
	13.	The Medical Officer.
	14.	The R.S.M.
	15.) 16)	War Diary.

War Diary

Rangers 12th London Regt

Volume III

March 1918

Instructions regarding War Diaries and Intelligence Summaries are contained in F. S. Regs., Part II. and the Staff Manual respectively. Title pages will be prepared in manuscript.

WAR DIARY
or
INTELLIGENCE SUMMARY.
(Erase heading not required.)

Army Form C. 2118.

Place	Date	Hour	Summary of Events and Information	Remarks and references to Appendices
LE EPINOIS SECTOR	1-3-18		HQ, C + D. Coys only moved to relieve 6th London Regt last night	
			A + B Coys remained at CHAUNY SUD in Divisional Reserve - The Companies found working parties for work on 175th Bde H.Q. and carried out Platoon Training -	
			Nothing of importance occurred during the day in the front line	
	2-3-18		"A" + "B" Coys moved to SINCENY and were employed burying cable, S of Butte de ROUY.	
		3.15am	Enemy bombarded the right front of the Battalion on our right (POST OFFICE RIFLES)	
			Nothing of importance occurred on our front -	
			Continuous noises of chopping, sawing + hammering were heard all day in the wood about H.12.a	
	3-3-18		G.O.C held conference of C.O's at Battalion H.Q. + afterwards visited posts held be our Left Company + those held by Right Coy. Q.V.R., the C.O. accompanying him -	
			The Battalion Lewis Gun + Bombing Schools commenced its first course (syllabus attached)	
			A + B Coys less personnel of School employed on burying cable as yesterday -	
			Nothing of importance occurred on our front.	
	4-3-18	12.5am	Sounds of a patrol action came from H.17.a.	
		1 am.	3 Germans approached P.P.6 from the Old Mill ~~working~~ and were firing on from the post. Two revolver shots were returned - A search discovered that a few strands of wire had been cut but no further evidence of enemy was found -	
		6 am	Heavy fall of snow commenced and continued until 9 am when a thaw commenced -	
		4.15pm	Hostile T.Ms fired 4 shells from H.11.d. on to H.11.c in front of our posts.	
			Usual sounds heard in enemy lines -	
			A + B Coys employed on burying cables as on previous day -	
	5-3-18		Very fine day and ground drying rapidly -	
			Usual enemy artillery activity, except that our forward areas received some attention + M G fire was directed on our forward posts from BRIQUENAY Farm + H.11.d.3.3 on our front posts.	

D. D. & L., London, E.C.
(A8004) Wt. W1771/M2631 750,000 5/17 Sch. 52 Forms/C2118/14

Instructions regarding War Diaries and Intelligence Summaries are contained in F. S. Regs., Part II. and the Staff Manual respectively. Title pages will be prepared in manuscript.

WAR DIARY
or
INTELLIGENCE SUMMARY.
(*Erase heading not required.*)

Army Form C. 2118.

Place	Date	Hour	Summary of Events and Information	Remarks and references to Appendices
LE EPINOIS SECTOR	5/3/18	3-5 pm	Enemy TM suspected at Mine Crater H.6.d.4.0.. Fired 7 LTM shells on H.11.a.	
		5.15 pm to 6.45 pm	Enemy heard chopping wood + hammering in area H.12 a	
		5-11 pm	Small single cylinder stationary engine heard.	
			Enemy OP. at H.12.a.5.8. approx was occupied throughout the day by one + sometimes two men	
		8 pm	L G's of A+B Coys relieved opposite numbers of "C+D" in front line -	
			A+B Coys employed burying cable as on previous day	~~Patrol reports.~~
	6-3-18	1-4.30 am	Three patrols sent out - ~~Reports attached~~ -	
		11.20 am	Man wearing peaked cap seen looking over wall of ruins of BRIQUENAY FARM.	
		12 pm	"A" Coy relieved "C" Coy in front line	O.O. 114
		4 pm	"B" Coy relieved "D" Coy in front line	
			Usual MG and Artillery activity - Usual sounds of chopping wood +c	~~Patrol Report~~
		6 pm	Patrol under Bn Intelligence Officer went out - ~~Report attached~~	~~Patrol Report~~
		9.30 pm	Patrol by "A" Coy sent out -	
			Very fine + sunny day with good observation -	
	7-3-18		C + D Coys (at SINCENY) bathing, cleaning up + interior economy	
			Increased activity by hostile artillery - Several shells (4.2's) in vicinity of Bn HQ.	
			Very fine day -	
			Patrols sent out by "A" Coy reports attached	Patrol Reports
	8-3-18	1 am	Patrol sent out by "B" Coy report attached	Patrol Report
			C+D Coys working on buried cable at the BUTTES.	
			Usual enemy activity.	
		6.15 pm	Patrol sent out by "A" Coy + Bn Scouts - Reports attached	Patrol Reports
			Very fine day	

D. D. & L., London, E.C.
(A8004) Wt. W1771/M2731 750,000 5/17 Sch. 52 Forms/C2118/14

Instructions regarding War Diaries and Intelligence Summaries are contained in F. S. Regs., Part II. and the Staff Manual respectively. Title pages will be prepared in manuscript.

WAR DIARY
or
INTELLIGENCE SUMMARY.
(Erase heading not required.)

Army Form C. 2118.

Place	Date	Hour	Summary of Events and Information	Remarks and references to Appendices
LE EPINOIS SECTOR	9/3/18	1 am	Patrol sent out by "B" Coy – Report attached –	Patrol Report.
			Quieter day than usual –	
			Very fine weather.	
		6 pm	Patrol sent out by "A" Coy – ~~Report attached~~ –	~~Patrol Report~~
		11 pm	Patrol sent out by "B" Coy – ~~ditto~~ –	~~ditto~~
	10-3-18		Patrol sent out – ditto –	– ditto –
	11-3-18		Lt Colonel A D. BAYLIFFE (M) went back to Brigade HQ to superintend training of Raiding Party. Major W. G WORTHINGTON MC arrived from Transport Lines to take over command of two Companies in the line –	
			Two patrols sent out during the night – Reports attached –	Patrol Reports
	12-3-18		Fine warm weather continues – "C" Coy relieved "A" Coy and "D" Coy (less special party) relieved "B" Coy in the front line	OO 115.
			3 Patrols sent out, but no signs of enemy –	
	13-3-18		Capt L.K SPENCER ~~again~~ patrolled the left Coy front – report attached –	Patrol Report
			2 Patrols on right reported nothing –	OO 116
	14-3-18		Lieut ~~K B~~ Clarke + 2/Lt W.B Wood went out with part of raiding party + encountered the enemy who appeared to be waiting for them – Report attached –	Patrol Report.
			A patrol which went out at 3 am to the same spot found no trace of the enemy –	
	15-3-18		German prisoner captured on front of Battalion on left stated that enemy were going to raid on that front on night of 15th or 16th	
			4 patrols went out covering "No Mans Land" at night but no signs of enemy –	Patrol Reports.
			Capt L.K SPENCER patrolled over ground for proposed raid – getting to within 30 yds of wood but found no signs of enemy – Report attached –	
	16-3-18		Patrols had nothing to report.	

D. D. & L., London, E.C.
(A8004) Wt. W1771/M2031 750,000 5/17 Sch. 52 Forms/C2118/14

Instructions regarding War Diaries and Intelligence Summaries are contained in F. S. Regs., Part II. and the Staff Manual respectively. Title pages will be prepared in manuscript.

WAR DIARY
or
INTELLIGENCE SUMMARY.
(Erase heading not required.)

Army Form C. 2118.

Place	Date	Hour	Summary of Events and Information	Remarks and references to Appendices
LE EPINOIS SECTOR	17-3-18		A Coy relieved "C" + "B" Coy relieved "D" in front line. On relief "C" Coy proceeded to the BUTTES DE ROUY until 12 mid. when they continued their way to SINCENY.	OO 116a
		5.30pm	Enemy was reported massing in SERVAIS on our left front – Our guns shelled the village with gas shells but at 12 midnight it was reported there was no enemy movement in SERVAIS – Otherwise quieter night than usual.	
	18-3-18		Two Companies QVR's relieved "A + B" Coys in front line. Battalion HQ relieved by "A" Coy + proceeded to SINCENY. "B" Coy into right position BATTLE ZONE.	OO 117
	19-3-18		Owing to new dispositions not being approved by ~~Higher Authority~~ III Corps "A" + "B" Coys took over front line again. Bn HQ less Major W G WORTHINGTON MC, 2nd Lt W E WOOD + 26 o.r. moved up to LA FORTELLE	OO 118.
	20-3-18		Fine weather – All quiet upon our front	
	21-3-18	4.45am	Bombardment started.	
		4.50am	Spoke to Brigade Major + told him nothing special happening on our front	
		4.55am	O C "D" Coy on 'phone, said nothing reported on left position – being shelled. (BUTTES [illegible] LOCALITY)	
		5 am	A + B Coys. report all quiet on their front.	
		5.22am	OC "A" Coy reports "All happy in front"	
		5.40am	Wired situation to Brigade –	
		5.50am	Enemy fire slackened on our front	
		6.10am	Received message from "D" Coy that heavy gas shell bombardment proceeding + he is moving platoons forward of it –	
		6.30am	Spoke to Adjutant QVR's on 'phone, who reported all quiet on their front –	
		6.40	"Blue Cross" Gas reported near Battalion HQ	
		6.55	Gas again smelt	
		7.25	Spoke to Brigade Major on phone + told him all quiet in front line + that ~~[illegible]~~ D Coy was free from gas that there were no casualties, also that situation on our left was same as here –	

D. D. & L., London, E.C.
(A8004) Wt. W1771/M2931 750,000 5/17 Sch. 52 Forms/C2118/14

Army Form C. 2118.

WAR DIARY
or
INTELLIGENCE SUMMARY.
(Erase heading not required.)

Instructions regarding War Diaries and Intelligence Summaries are contained in F. S. Regs., Part II. and the Staff Manual respectively. Title pages will be prepared in manuscript.

Place	Date	Hour	Summary of Events and Information	Remarks and references to Appendices
LE EPINOIS SECTOR	21-3-18	7.40 am	2/Lieut E.W. WOOD reported as liaison from Brigade – He reported all well at BUTTES.	
		7.50 "	Liaison Officer reported from 7th LONDON REGT on right flank & reports "alls well"	
		8.10 "	2/Lieut E.W. WOOD left for 9th LONDON REGT.	
		8.30 "	O.C "A" Coy reported he was taking special precautions and message to that effect is on its way	
		8.45 "	Reported to Brigade that night positions are manned during mist & patrols out report all quiet	
		9.55 "	Brigade Major said over phone, that BEAUTOR (T.30d.) was surrounded by enemy & that this information was to be repeated to the 9th LONDON REGT. and tell them to watch marsh carefully and send out their usual wire patrols with Lewis guns. Also that they were to report situation half hourly and use their Power Buzzer. – Sent message to the above effect to the 9th LONDON REGT.	
		10.45 "	Received message from Brigade to "Man Battle positions"	
		11.35 "	OC "B" Coy reports all quiet.	
		12.5 pm	OC "B" Coy reports about 20 enemy opposite his centre post	
		12.30 "	Message from OC "A" Coy that party of 25 enemy seen descending hill at H.11.c.95.75 to H.11.c.80.60 and then take cover.	
			Spoke to OC "A" Coy who said he was sending out to investigate –	
			He thought the enemy had been surprised by the clearance of the mist –	
		12.50 "	Gunner Liaison Officer returned from visiting "A" Coy and said that a report had come through from 9th LONDON REGT that enemy had been bombing their P.P. line –	
		12.55 "	Spoke to Adjutant 9th LON REGT who said that about a hour ago some enemy were tampering with his wire, but had been stopped also that there had been some bombing of his P.P.'s.	
		1.15 pm	Reported to Brigade – situation quiet on Battalion front –	
		2.10 "	– ditto – – ditto –	
		3.40 "	– ditto – – ditto –	
			O.C. "A" Coy reported all quiet.	
		4.10 "	Received report from OC "A" Coy.	
		6.15 "	Reported to Brigade all quiet.	

D. D. & L., London, E.C.
(A8004) Wt. W1771/M2731 750,000 5/17 Sch. 52 Forms/C2118/14

Instructions regarding War Diaries and Intelligence Summaries are contained in F. S. Regs., Part II. and the Staff Manual respectively. Title pages will be prepared in manuscript.

WAR DIARY
or
INTELLIGENCE SUMMARY.
(Erase heading not required.)

Army Form C. 2118.

Place	Date	Hour	Summary of Events and Information	Remarks and references to Appendices
LE EPINOIS SECTOR	21-3-18	8 pm	Brigade Major rang up to say that S.O.S. had gone up on boundary of our Bn and the 9th LONDON. On communicating with O.C. "B" Coy + 9th LON REGT HQ they report they know nothing of it –	
		8.3.	S.O.S. seen to go up at bearing S W magnetic	
		8.15.	Reported to Brigade all quiet	
		9.15.	Reported to Brigade all quiet	
		9.30.	Rations arrived.	
		10.45.	Reported to Brigade all quiet	
		11.45.	Reported to Brigade situation quiet	
	22-3-18	1.30 am	9th LONDON REGT report 3 prisoners captured of the 13th Division (GERMAN)	
		1.45.	Reported to Brigade situation quiet	
		3.30.	Sentry post at Red House reports Gas Shells in direction of AMIGNY-ROUY	
		3.45	Reported to Brigade, situation quiet + gas shells mentioned above –	
		6 am	Reported to Brigade situation quiet	
		8 am	– ditto –	
		8.50.	A + B Coys report enemy T.M. active on picquet line	
		8.55	Reported this to Brigade	
		9 am	9th LONDON REGT report 2 more prisoners who state their Regt was shelled + scattered on the DOUILLET-BEAUTOR road	
		10.17.	Increased activity by our artillery –	
		10.30	Brigade Major informed us on phone that B.G.C. on way to these HQ. and asked us to give him following information on arrival, viz:- "Corps states that enemy intend to attack today at junction of French + British Armies with a strength of 10 Divisions on a front of 15 Kilometres and the attack to be pushed to a depth of 10 Kilos" Brigade Major said that reinforcements were coming up behind us –	
		10.50.	B.G.C. arrived + was given above information on which he returned at once to Bde HQ.	
		11 am	Reported to Brigade "Situation quiet"	
		12 noon	– ditto –	
		1 pm	– ditto –	
		2 pm	– ditto –	

D. D. & L., London, E.C.
(A8004) Wt. W1771/M2-31 750,000 5/17 Sch. 52 Forms/C2118/14

Instructions regarding War Diaries and Intelligence Summaries are contained in F. S. Regs., Part II. and the Staff Manual respectively. Title pages will be prepared in manuscript.

WAR DIARY
or
INTELLIGENCE SUMMARY.
(*Erase heading not required.*)

Army Form C. 2118.

Place	Date	Hour	Summary of Events and Information	Remarks and references to Appendices
LE EPINOIS SECTOR	22-3-18	2.10pm	Rang up 9th LONDON REGT & asked for information	
			Increased artillery mixed with MG fire on our front	
		2.35pm	Rang up 9th LONDON REGT who reported that it was not on their front	
		2.45	Gas shell fell near Bn HQ	
		3.15	Reported to Brigade "Situation quiet"	
		3.30	Received wire from Brigade that TERGNIER held by us two enemy in village –	
		4.30	Brigade Major reported on phone that enemy reported putting a lot of smoke into AMIGNY-ROUY	
		5.50	and on a line from thence to CONDREN – He would obtain confirmation + let us know –	
		6.15	Reported to Brigade all quiet –	
		6 pm	A shell like black shrapnel burst above Bn HQ somewhat high up + scattered a black substance which emitted smoke on reaching the ground – The substance dissolves into moisture + possesses no smell –	
		6.20	Capt SPENCER called in + reported that there was a quantity of gas in The wood behind LA FORTELLE	
		7.15	Reported to Brigade "All quiet"	
		7.30	Fires observed burning at E. base of S BUTTE.	
			A "dud" shell found near Red House description as follows:– Calibre 3" length 15½" weight 18 lbs approx.– Marking on fuse 95 E (F). 17 FKZ 17 ZIE GUSS T – On shell 614 z KP 17	
			Reported description to Brigade 1.0 and asked for instructions as to disposal –	
		8.15	Reported to Brigade – Situation quiet –	
		9.15	– ditto –	
		9.20	Bde report TERGNIER in enemy hands, CONDREN threatened – Reserve Coy of 10th LONDON REGT has been sent to take up position facing N. at OLD WHARF (B 25 b 5.8) + send out strong patrols to CONDREN	
		9.30	Brigade report 125th FRENCH Division have arrived in Divisional Sector – preliminary dispositions 2 Bns N of CHAUNY, 2 Bns about OGNES – 2 Bns S of OISE in area SINCENY-BICHANCOURT – Artillery, one group (3 batteries) about SINCENY, 2 groups (6 batteries) between CHAUNY & VILLEQUIER AUMONT	
		10.15	Reported to Brigade situation quiet –	

D. D. & L., London, E.C.
(A8004) Wt. W1771/M2-31 750,000 5/17 Sch. 52 Forms/C2118/14

Army Form C. 2118.

WAR DIARY
or
INTELLIGENCE SUMMARY.
(Erase heading not required.)

Instructions regarding War Diaries and Intelligence Summaries are contained in F. S. Regs., Part II. and the Staff Manual respectively. Title pages will be prepared in manuscript.

Place	Date	Hour	Summary of Events and Information	Remarks and references to Appendices
L^E EPINOIS SECTOR	22-3-18	10.30 pm	Captain BEST MC & Lieut ANDERSON arrived at Battn HQ to discuss plans for re-distribution of Companies	
		10.45 "	C.O. spoke to B M - re-distribution scheme cancelled -	
		11.15 "	Reported to Bde - Situation quiet -	
	23-3-18	12.15 AM	- ditto -	
		12.25 "	Bde report quiet on front - Patrol of 9th LONDON REGT returned from CONDREN at 11pm reports garrison intact & in good heart. Enemy cavalry patrols approached their positions during day and were disposed of -	
		1.15 "	Reported to Brigade Situation quiet -	
		2.30 "	- ditto -	
		4.15 "	- ditto - no wind -	
		5.00 "	Brigade informs us:- "125th FRENCH DIV are making a counter attack this morning with the object of driving the enemy across" "CROZAT CANAL & re-establishing our line on western bank of Canal. - Artillery bombardment is to" "commence at 6am - Infantry attack at 7am"	
		5.45	Reported to Bde Situation quiet -	
		7 am	- ditto -	
		8 am	- ditto -	
		8.30	Congratulations of "C in C" received	
		9 am 10 am 11 am	Reported to Bde "Situation quiet"	
		11.40 "	Reported to Bde that piece of base of 8" Armour piercing shell base action fuse had fallen on road between Foresters' House & AMIGNY ROUY - Believed to be portion of shell seen to burst on R. BUTTE	
		12 noon 1 pm 2 " 3 " 4 " 5 " 6 " 7 "	Situation quiet - Reported to Brigade	
		7 pm	Brigade Major rang up to say that proposed alteration of left flank suggested yesterday was definitely cancelled -	

D. D. & L., London, E.C.
(A8004) Wt. W1771/M2-31 750,000 5/17 Sch. 52 Forms/C2118/14

Army Form C. 2118.

Instructions regarding War Diaries and Intelligence Summaries are contained in F. S. Regs., Part II. and the Staff Manual respectively. Title pages will be prepared in manuscript.

WAR DIARY
or
INTELLIGENCE SUMMARY.
(Erase heading not required.)

Place	Date	Hour	Summary of Events and Information	Remarks and references to Appendices
Le EPINOIS SECTOR	23-3-18	8 PM	Reported situation quiet to Brigade	
		9 "	- ditto -	
		9.20 "	Enemy 'plane overhead - dropped lights over AMIGNY-ROUY	
		10 PM	Reported to Bde - Situation quiet -	
		10.25	O.C. Coy BUTTES Right locality phoned that he could hear rifle + Lewis gun fire on his left which sounded near - Reassured him -	OO 119 attached
		11 PM	Reported to Bde situation quiet	
		11.30	Salvo by enemy guns of small calibre apparently directed on BUTTES	
		11.35	BM rang up to know whether this shelling was on our front + explained accordingly -	
	24-3-18	12.5 AM	Reported to Brigade situation quiet	
		12.30 "	TM's heard firing on Bn Front - Rang up R & L front companies - L. Coy alright, - R. Coy say it is on their front	
		12.37	T.M's ceased	
		12.50 "	Observer from TREE POST No2 reported 160 Heavy TMs fired at PP1. - M.G & L.G fire heard from direction of P.P.2.	
		12.55 "	R Front Coy report all quiet	
		1.5 "	Reported Bde - Situation quiet -	
		2 AM	Received message from Bde:- "During the night the area held by the Division is to be strengthened by 3 FRENCH Divisions" "2 north of CHAUNY & 1 SOUTH complete with artillery (37 guns) is to hold the GREEN LINE between" "the present Divisional Right Boundary + the river - The line as held by this Brigade will therefore" "remain unchanged"	
			Reported to Bde - situation quiet -	
			- ditto -	
		3 AM	Brigade phoned asking situation - replied "Quiet" - Bde said line with ULLESWATER discontinued -	
		3.50 "	Reported to Bde - situation quiet on our front - no wind -	
		4 AM	Asked "B" Coy to report at once any disturbance on left -	
		4.15 "		
		5.15 " 6.5 " 7.45 " 9.30 "	Reported to Brigade - "Situation quiet"	

D. D. & L., London, E.C. (A8004) Wt. W1771/M2731 750,000 5/17 Sch. 52 Forms/C2118/14

Instructions regarding War Diaries and Intelligence Summaries are contained in F. S. Regs., Part II. and the Staff Manual respectively. Title pages will be prepared in manuscript.

WAR DIARY
or
INTELLIGENCE SUMMARY.
(Erase heading not required.)

Army Form C. 2118.

Place	Date	Hour	Summary of Events and Information	Remarks and references to Appendices
1E EPINOIS SECTOR	24/3/18	10.25 AM	Brigade reported that N. of the Brigade on our left the enemy have pierced the CHAUNY-VILLEQUIER-AUMONT road - Bridges at CHAUNY have been ~~destroyed~~ blown up - French are continuing our defensive flank Westward from SINCENY covering southern exits of CHAUNY VILLAGE -	
		11.45 "	Bde report move of their HQ in progress - Old HQ remaining open until completion of move - BM told me to report this to 9th & 10th LONDON REGT the latter to report to MGC. & T.M.B.	
			Our Transport Lines have also moved -	
		12.10 pm	BM informed us on 'phone that 10TH LONDON REGT were moving their Company from AMIGNY-ROUY to BUTTES to strengthen position there -	
		12.15 "	Reported to Bde, situation quiet	
		12.50 "	Received wire from Brigade that their new HQ opened at PIERREMANDE -	
		1 PM, 2 ", 3 "	Reported to Bde: situation quiet	
		3.20 "	Spoke to 9th LONDON REGT who report CONDREN occupied by the enemy	
		4 pm	Reported to Bde "Situation quiet" Wind 5 MPH	
		5 pm	- ditto -	
		5.30 "	Received orders from Brigade as to re-distribution and called meeting of Company Commanders to explain it -	
		6 pm	Reported to Brigade, situation quiet	
		7 pm	- ditto -	
		7.15 pm	Brigade Major called and explained situation -	
		8 pm, 9 pm, 10 pm, 11 pm	Reported to Bde situation. Quiet.	

D. D. & L., London, E.C.
(A8004) Wt. W1771/M2031 750,000 5/17 Sch. 52 Forms/C2118/14

Instructions regarding War Diaries and Intelligence Summaries are contained in F. S. Regs., Part II. and the Staff Manual respectively. Title pages will be prepared in manuscript.

WAR DIARY
or
INTELLIGENCE SUMMARY.
(Erase heading not required.)

Army Form C. 2118.

Place	Date	Hour	Summary of Events and Information	Remarks and references to Appendices
Le EPINOIS SECTOR	24-3-18	11.30pm	Relief complete reported to Bde	
		12 midnt	Reported to Bde. situation quiet.	
	25-3-18	1 am.	-do-	
		2 am.	-do-	
		3.45am.	-do-	
		5 am	-do-	
		6 am.	-do-	
		7 am.	-do-	
		8 am.	-do-	
		8.20am	Heavy artillery fire from direction of CHAUNY.	
		9 am.	Fire still continuing. Adjutant ULLESWATER reported quiet night on his front. Reported to Bde. situation quiet on our front.	
		9.15am	Noise of heavy firing growing fainter.	
		12 noon	C.O. met G.O.C. Brigade at H.Q. Right Buttes Locality.	
		2.30pm.	Bn H.Q. moved to Right Buttes Locality leaving forward echelon at LA FORTELLE.	
		5pm.	Reported situation quiet to Bde.	
		6pm.	-do-	
		6.15pm.	Spoke to Burnside (found Bn H.Q.) re report collected by our patrol from ULLESWATER Right Coy. He said there was no information and doubted its accuracy.	
		6.20pm.	Spoke to Adjutant ULLESWATER about it, who said he did not think that there were any enemy on the ST. GOBAIN Road, but in any case our artillery were dealing with them.	
		6.35pm.	Spoke to Burnside and ordered all notice boards to be removed in the wood, and forward telephone not to go further than Arlette Post.	
		7.30pm.	S.O.S. sent up from our Bn. front. 200 Bosch reported in H.11.b.6.5.	
		7.40pm.	Spoke to Burnside, and told him to let me know when artillery could cease.	
		7.45pm.	Spoke to ULLESWATER who said he had put up S.O.S. Told him that all seemed quiet on our front.	
		7.50pm.	Spoke to Spencer, who said the map reference H.11.b.6.5. was not correct but enemy were seen in No Man's Land N. of BRIQUENAY FARM.	
		8pm.	Enemy started shelling N. edge of wood near Bn. H.Q., and also shelled Buttes with 5.9 shells.	
		8.10pm	Capt. Burnside reported all correct on our front.	
		9pm to 5am.	Continuous shelling of neighbourhood of Bn. H.Q. by enemy heavy guns.	
	26-3-18	9 am.	Party of four men, believed to be Bosch seen in Laie Servais near Seven Dials. Spencer took L.G. and team to investigate. Small numbers of enemy definitely reported in wood during the day. A patrol of 12 Other Ranks from D Coy. and Bn. Scouts went out from P.3. in the early morning and failed to return. Reported hourly to Bde. on situation.	

D. D. & L., London, E.C.
(A8004) Wt. W1771/M2 31 750,000 5/17 Sch. 52 Forms/C2118/14

WAR DIARY
or
INTELLIGENCE SUMMARY.
(Erase heading not required.)

Place	Date	Hour	Summary of Events and Information	Remarks and references to Appendices
LE EPINOIS SECTOR	26-3-18.	3pm.	Conference of B.G.C. and C.Os. at Buttes de Rouy to discuss withdrawal from present position.	
		5pm	Orders for withdrawal received.	
		8pm.	Zero hour. "C" Coy. and 2 platoons "D" Coy., the whole under Capt. L.K. Spencer remained – C Coy. in its same positions, 2 platoons D Coy in LA FORTELLE. 10 platoons of Q.V.R. remain in AMIGNY ROUY localities and the whole force under the command of O.C. Q.V.R. with H.Q. at Buttes de Rouy.	
			Order of march of Bn: "B" Coy., H.Q., "A" Coy, 2 platoons "D" Coy. O.O. 120 attached.	O.O.120.
			Companies got away without difficulty or casualties. On arrival at AUTREVILLE Companies were diverted to BAC D'ARBLINCOURT. H.Q. arrived about 12 midnight. 6 platoons Q.V.R. were attached to the Bn. to replace the 6 platoons of Rangers left in LA FORTELLE sector. On arrival Bn. came under orders of 173 Inf. Bde.	
ABBECOURT SECTOR	27-3-18		Situation Quiet. Ordered to be in readiness to relieve French troops in the front line tonight.	
		8pm	Orders to relieve arrived. "A" + "B" Coys. with Composite Coy. (2 platoons D Coy Rangers and 2 platoons Q.V.R.) in support took over from French (246th and 204th). Relief complete 3 am. Front – between River OISE and MARIZELLE-MANICAMP road from G.7.d.7.8. to III.21.a.7.6. Q.V.R. Coy. took over from B Coy. along S. side of AILETTE River from L.30.c.2.3., exclusive to L.27.b.5.6. Bn. H.Q. at BAC D'ARBLINCOURT.	
	28-3-18		O.C. A Coy reported that the French Coy. on his right had left without being relieved and his right flank was accordingly open. A platoon of the support Coy. was sent to cover the gap and patrols sent out to get touch. The 16th Entrenching Bn. were found to be on our right with 2 Coys. in CHAUNY SUD.	
			Situation quiet. Between 5 and 6 pm some shelling of junction of OISE and AISNE Canal and River OISE. A few shells about BAC D'ARBLINCOURT during the day.	
	29-3-18		OISE rose about 2 feet 6 ins. during 24 hours.	
		9 am.	A large dump, apparently S.A.A. was observed burning in ABBECOURT. Situation quiet.	
		9pm	Patrols of A Coy. report enemy transport distinctly heard in front of Coy. area at the gallop. Believed to be on MAREST-OGNES-CHAUNY road. Reported to Bde.	
	30-3-18		The river bank was patrolled throughout the night. All quiet: nothing to report.	
			"C" Coy + H.Q. and 2 platoons "D" Coy. rejoined the Bn. and relieved the 6 platoons of the Q.V.R. who returned to their unit. Relief complete about midnight.	
			"A" Coy. 18th Entrenching Bn. occupied a position on S. side of OISE + AISNE Canal facing N. with left flank on junction of CANAL and River AILETTE at L.30.c.1.3., coming under orders of O.C. Rangers.	
	31-3-18	7am.	O.C. A Coy. reported that S.O.S. had gone up at CHAUNY SUD. Bn. stood to.	
			Further report from O.C. A Coy. states that a patrol of the 16th Entrenching Bn. on our right was	

D. D. & L., London, E.C.
(A8004) Wt. W1771/M2731 750,000 5/17 Sch. 52 Forms/C2118/14

Instructions regarding War Diaries and Intelligence Summaries are contained in F. S. Regs., Part II. and the Staff Manual respectively. Title pages will be prepared in manuscript.

WAR DIARY
or
INTELLIGENCE SUMMARY.
(Erase heading not required.)

Army Form C. 2118.

Place	Date	Hour	Summary of Events and Information	Remarks and references to Appendices
ABBECOURT SECTOR	31-3-1918		attacked and forced to retire. He took out a patrol and found the 16th Entrenching Bn. in a skirmishing action with the enemy, who now hold Viaduct at G. 23. b. 80.40. (CHAUNY SUD). Our line approximately G.8.a.5.5. to G.3.c.00.40. to G.3.c.40.30. Keeping in touch with the situation by patrols.	
		11.am.	Bn. stood down.	
			The 16th Entrenching Bn. report that they captured 24 prisoners with an M.G. this morning. 16th Entrenching Bn. counter-attacked this afternoon, recapturing position lost this morning. Took further 56 prisoners and 2 M.Gs.	
		7.30pm	Reported to Bde. situation quiet.	
		8pm	Large fire observed at CHAUNY.	
			"D" Coy. relieved "A" Coy. in front line.	
		12 midnt	Relief complete.	
			1st April. 1918.	
			A A Bayliffe Lieut-Colonel. Comdg. "The Rangers" 12th London Regiment.	

D. D. & L., London, E.C.
(A8004) Wt. W1771/M2731 750,000 5/17 Sch. 52 Forms/C2118/14

Secret. The Rangers. Copy No. 15

Operation Order No 119.

Ref. Map [illegible] N.W. 1/20,000

1. Unless instructions are received to the contrary an inter-Company relief will be carried out tomorrow night, 24/25th March. The relief will be carried out after dark and movement will not take place until receipt of the message "Carry on" from Battalion H.Q.
"C" Coy. will relieve "A" Coy. and "D" Company "B" Coy. and vice versa.
Details to be arranged between Company Commanders concerned. Commanders of "B" and "D" Coys. will meet at Bn. H.Q. at 10am tomorrow for this purpose after which time table will be issued.
2. Lists of ammunition and trench stores taken over will be forwarded to Bn. H.Q. as soon as possible after relief.
3. Completion of relief will be notified to Bn. H.Q. by wiring Coy. Commander's name.
4. Acknowledge.

H. Cole Lt.
Lt. & Adjt.
The Rangers.

Issued at
23-3-1918.

[illegible] Operation Orders [illegible] 5

After ZERO hour to be notified later the following [illegible] will [illegible]

1. 'C' Coy. & 2 Platoons 'D' Coy. will [illegible] the command of [illegible] and will come under the orders of O.C. ULLESWATER whose H.Q. will be at the BUTTES.

2. 'C' Coy. will remain in its present position. 2 platoons 'D' Coy. will remain [illegible] garrison of LA FORTELLE.

3. The Battalion less C. Coy. & 2 platoons D Coy. will move by [illegible] route by [illegible] to AUTREVILLE where guides will meet them & conduct them to BESME.

4. The route to be followed will be [illegible] BUTTES [illegible] keep to [illegible] roads H.8.c.10.25 – H.13.c. 95.45 – G.24.d.50.80 – G.17.d. 50.75 & thence to AUTREVILLE cross roads G.12.a.1.4., where guides will be met.

5. Lewis ~~[illegible]~~ guns & 20 pans ammunition per gun will be carried to AUTREVILLE where it is hoped limbers will be met.

6. As much transport as can be arranged for will be [illegible] to-night to bring away surplus stores of L.G. ammunition, etc. If the limbers

have not arrived before the move takes place the surplus stores will be dumped ready for loading under 2 men for security & a reliable N.C.O. to be found by "A" Coy. "A" & "D" Coys. will dump at LA FORTELLE and by "B" Coy. at their present ration dump.

7. Blankets will be carried on the man.

8. Complete silence and strictest march discipline will be maintained throughout the move.

[illegible] B[illegible] [illegible]
ZERO DAY [illegible]
ZERO [illegible]

[illegible]/9/18. [illegible]

Capt & Adjt.

7.10 pm

[illegible]

Distribution.

Copy No. 1 Retained.
2 175th Inf. Bde.
3 Maj. Worthington M.C.
4 O.C. A Coy.
5 B
6 C
7 D
8 HQ
9 Q.V.R.
10 7th Londons.
11 The Medical Officer.
12 The Transport Officer.
13 The Quartermaster.
14 R.S.M.
15 War Diary.

"The Rangers" 12th London Regt

BATTALION BOMBING AND GRENADE SCHOOL

Course 2ndMarch to 7th March 1918

INSTRUCTORS

"A" Coy - L/Sgt. H. MAKEPEACE. - "B" Coy.

L/c W. BOND. L/c J.A.BRODIE

TRAINING GROUND.............SINCENY

TRAINING PROGRAMME

First Day	9.00 - 9.30	Inspection parade and march to training ground
	9.30 -10.30	Lecture. Importance of bombing and general subjects.
	10.30 -11.00	P.T.
	11.15 -12.15	Instruction in mechanism of Mills No.5. & 23.
	1.55 pm	Parade on Training Ground.
	2.00 - 3.00	Practice in throwing Mills No.5. and firing dummy 23.
Second Day	9.00 - 9.30	Inspection parade and march to training ground.
	9.30 -10.30.	Lecture. Organisation & tactics of bombers.
	10.30 -11.00	Throwing from trench.
	11.15 -12.15	Throwing live.
	1.55 pm	Parade on Training Ground.
	2.00 - 3.00	Live firing No.23.
Third Day	9.00 - 9.30.	Inspection and march to training ground.
	9.30 -10.30	Trench work practice.
	10.30 -11.00	Throwing practice.
	11.15 -12.15	Lectures on No. 24 and 22.
	1.55 pm	Parade on Training Ground.
	2.00 - 3.00	Firing live No. 24
	8.00 - 9.00	Preliminary night attack practice with dummy
Fourth Day	9.00 - 9.30.	Inspection and march to training ground.
	9.30 -10.30	Lectures, barricades etc.
	10.30 -11.00	Throwing.
	11.15 -12.15	Trench attack with live.
	1.55 pm	Parade on Training Ground.
	2.00 - 3.00	German Grenades.
Fifth Day	9.00 - 9.30	Inspection and march to training ground.
	9.30 -10.30.	Oral examination.
	10.30 -11.00	Throwing.
	11.15 -12.15	Practical Tests.
	1.55 pm	Parade on Training Ground.
	2.00 - 3.00	Live throwing.
	8.00 - 9.00	Attack on Trenches.

[signature]

Captain
"The Rangers" 12th Ldn Regt

1.3.18

"The Rangers" 12th London Regiment

BATTALION BOMBING AND GRENADE SCHOOL

Course 2nd March to 7th March 1918

INSTRUCTORS

"A" COY L/SGT. H. MAKEPEACE "B" COY

Training Ground ....SINCENY

TRAINING PROGRAMME.

First Day	9.00 - 9.30	Inspection parade and march to Training Ground.
	9.30 - 10.30	Lecture. Importance of Bombing and general subjects.
	10.30 - 11.00	P.T.
	11.15 - 12.15	Instruction in Mechanism of Mills No.5. & 23.
	1.55 pm	Parade on Training Ground.
	2,00 - 3.00	Practice in throwing Mills No.5. and firing dummy 23.
Second Day	9.00 - 9.30	Inspection parade and march to training Grd.
	9.30 - 10.30	Lecture. Organisation and tactics of bombers
	10.30 - 11.00	Throwing from Trench
	11.15 - 12.15	Throwing Live.
	1.55 pm	Parade on Training Ground
	2.00 - 3.00	Live firing No.23.
Third Day	9.00 - 9.30	Inspection and march to training Ground.
	9.30 - 10.30	Trench work practice.
	10.30 - 11.00	Throwing practice.
	11.15 - 12.15	Lecture on No. 24 and 22.
	1.55 pm	Parade on Training Ground.
	2.00 - 3.00	Firing live 24. practice
	8.00 - 9.00	Preliminary night attack/with dummy
Fourth Day	9.00 - 9.30	Inspection and march to training Ground.
	9.30 - 10.30	Lecture. Barricades etc.
	10.30 - 11.00	Throwing.
	11.15 - 12.15	Trench attack with live.
	1.55 pm	Parade on training Ground.
	2.00 - 3.00	German greandes.
Fifth Day	9.00 - 9.30	Inspection and march to Training Ground.
	9.30 - 10.30	Oral Examination.
	10.30 - 11.00	Throwing.
	11.15 - 12.15	Practical tests.
	1.55 pm	Parade on training Ground.
	2.00 - 3.00	Live throwing.
	8.00 - 9.00	Attack on Trenches.

(Signed) V.L.BURNSIDE
Capt
"The Rangers" 12th Ldn Regt.

1.3.18

Copy No. ...16......

[illegible] Rangers.

OPERATION ORDER No. 114.

Ref. Sheet [illegible] 1/20,000.

1. "A" Company will relieve "D" Company and "B" Company will relieve "C" Company in the line to-morrow 9th. March 1918. "C" & "D" Companies will take over billets in [illegible] from their opposite Companies.

2. Companies will move by half Platoons at 10 minutes interval, the first half Platoon of "A" Company passing road junction at G.11.c.30.35 at [illegible] p.m. First half Platoon of "B" Company at 2 p.m. They will be met by guides at cross tracks H.7.a.50,40.

3. Two guides per Platoon and 1 per Coy. Hd.Qrs. will report at Bn. Hd.Qrs.; "D" Company at 9.30 a.m. - "C" Coy. at 1.30 p.m.

4. Lewis Guns and magazines of "A" & "B" Companies, accompanied by No.s 1 & 2 of each gun will be sent up to-night with the ration column. These guns will take the place of "C" & "D" Companies guns in the line and as soon as they are in position "C" & "D" Coys. guns will be withdrawn. These, together with the magazines, and accompanied by No. 1 & 2 of each gun, will be taken back on the limbers. On arrival at [illegible] the gun numbers will report to the O.C. their opposite Coy. under whose orders they will remain for the night. O.C. "A" & "B" Companies will arrange for the exchange of magazines, taking care that the gun positions are not denuded during the process.

5. Blankets will remain as Trench and Billet stores and will be duly taken over. Officers' baggage of "A" & "B" Coys. will come up with the ration limbers to-morrow night under arrangements to be made between O.C. Coys. and the Transport Officer and that of "C" & "D" Coys. returned by the same means.

6. Completion of relief will be notified to Bn. Hd.Qrs. by Coy. Commdrs. in person.

7. ACKNOWLEDGE.

(Sgd) [illegible] Clarke, Capt.
A/Adjt. "The Rangers".

8th. March 1918.

Issued at ....

Copy No. 1 Retained.
2 175th. Inf. Bde.
3 9th. Londons.
4 7th. Londons.
5 18th. Londons.
6 Major [illegible].G.Worthington, [illegible].
7 O.C. "A" Coy.
8 "B"
9 "C"
10 "D"
11 Hd.Qrs.
12 The Transport Officer.
13 The Quartermaster.
14 The Medical Officer.
15 The R.S.M
16 War Diary.
17

[illegible] ....

[illegible]

[illegible]

[illegible] - [illegible]

Ref. Sheet 7[illegible] . 1[illegible],[illegible],[illegible].

BRIGADE DISTRIBUTION. 1. (a) The 17[illegible]th. Infantry Brigade Sector consists of two zones of defence.
1. The Forward Zone.
2. The Battle Zone.
These Zones are continued on the right by the flanking Brigade. On the left the bed of the River [illegible] and the marshland bordering it, is unheld. This forms a gap of [illegible] yards in the forward zone and [illegible] yards in the Battle Zone between our positions and the Brigade on this flank.

(b) The Forward Zone is intended to give warning of an enemy attack and to break it up.

(c) The Battle Zone is the position on which an enemy attack on a large scale will be contested and on which the last reserves of the Brigade will be employed if necessary.

(d) The Garrison of the forward zone consists of :-
On the Right.
1 Battalion (less [illegible] Companies in Divl. Reserve)
[illegible] Vickers Machine Guns.
On the Left.
1 Battalion.
[illegible] Vickers Machine Guns.

(e) The Garrison of the Battle Zone consists of :-
1 Battalion.
1 Company Pioneers.
[illegible] Vickers Machine Guns.

(f) In addition to the above one section Vickers Machine Guns, located at [illegible] of the [illegible] holding the Battle Zone, is in Divisional Reserve.

[illegible] DISTRIBUTION. 2 The attached map shows the boundaries of the [illegible] front which extends from [illegible] road (inclusive) in the North to [illegible] ATTE (inclusive) in the South.
The defence of this sector is organised in depth and comprises :-
(a) [illegible] line on [illegible]
[illegible]

[illegible]

(b) Picquet Line, comprising [illegible] Posts numbered from right to left [illegible]

(c) Support Line.

(d) The Keep at [illegible].

2. The above front is divided into 2 Coys. [illegible] with Bn. H.Q.r. Coy. as garrison to [illegible]. Each Coy. holds its area in depth the right Coy. having two Platoons in the Picquet Line and 2 in the Support line, the left Coy. having 1 Platoon in the Picquet line and 3 Platoons in the support line.

3. Each of the forward Platoons furnishes night sentries on the Observation line. The Right Support Platoon of the left Coy. furnishes the garrison for Post [illegible] in the Picquet line and this garrison furnishes the observation line Post P.[illegible].
The left support Platoon of the Left Coy. furnishes the garrison for Post P.6 in the picquet line and this garrison furnishes sentries for the Observation line Post [illegible].

LEWIS GUNS 3. In addition to 1 Lewis Gun per Platoon, each Coy. has an extra Lewis Gun which is treated as a Trench Store and handed over to the Coys. from Divisional Reserve on relief. The H.Qrs. Coy. has two further Lewis Guns which are normally mounted for Anti-Aircraft Defence and are available to reinforce the garrison of [illegible] in the event of an enemy attack.

MACHINE GUNS 4. 1 at [illegible] [illegible].25.30 and 1 at [illegible]

ARTILLERY BARRAGE 5. Line is shown ~~in yellow~~ on attached map.

ACTION IN CASE OF ATTACK. 6. (a) On receipt from Bn. H.Qrs. of message "Prepare for attack" or in the event of [illegible] being sent up on the Brigade front :-

(i) Garrisons of Posts will stand to in their shelters or dug-outs if no hostile attack has developed upon Bn. front. They will ascertain the extent of their flanks reporting any information, either positive or negative to Bn. H.Qrs. via their Coy. H.Qrs.
Extra vigilance will be maintained.
No troops will be employed for work other than on their own Battle Fighting Posts.
If by night listening patrols will be sent out 1 hour before dawn and remain out 1 hour after dawn.

(ii) On receipt of message from Bn. H.Qrs. "Man Battle Stations" all Coys. will immediately do so, reporting to Bn. H.Qrs. when dispositions are complete.
Working parties or other units which happen to be [illegible]

- 5 -

In the [illegible] locality in which they are [illegible] the officer in charge [illegible] to [illegible].

PRINCIPLE OF DEFENCE 7. In the event of attack each platoon will hold its ground until the last. No posts will be reinforced nor can any reinforcements be expected from the Battle Zone the role of the garrisons of the Forward zone being to delay the enemy as long as possible to enable the Battle zone to be manned and defence organized there. Garrisons must therefore stand their ground even though their flanks be turned and all posts must be so organized as to be capable of all round defence.
It should be borne in mind that the enemy will be fighting in a wood with which he is unfamiliar and which is thickly wired at all important points and he will have no accurate knowledge of the points where resistance will be met with. We, on the other hand know our ground and what we intend to do. Consequently to attempt to manoeuvre our own troops in the wood during the course of the enemy attack would only tend to confuse our arrangements for defence without gaining any material advantage over the enemy.

(Sgd.) [illegible] Clarke, Lieut.
Adjt. "The Rangers"
12th. London Regt..

6th. March 1918.

Issued at ....

Copy No. 1 Retained.
2 175th. Inf. Bde.
3 O.C. "A" Coy.
4 "B"
5 "C"
6 "D"
7 H.Q.[illegible].
8 The Medical Officer.
9 The R.[illegible].
10
11 War Diary.

Patrol Report for night 7/8 March 1918.

Patrol Leader (Name) 2/Lt Hilton Strength O.R. 4 Hours when out. 1.15 to 3.45.	Orders given to patrol & by whom	Information obtained Route taken	Remarks of Patrol leader (Regt of prisoners - enemy patrols met offensive action taken etc.
	To obtain Identification by Capt Best	Left the line at H5.d.5.7 but unable to get through the wire as apparently there were no gaps. Patrol tried to get thro. on road & after difficulty managed to do so. The wood adjoining road is well protected by obstacles, trip wires & barbed wire. The road by H5d 57 is well barricaded to the depth of about 80' with obstacles trip wires & barbed wire. After an hour and a half patrol proceeded up the road towards Brquenay Farm but no enemy Scouts or patrols were encountered. I waited until 3.45 & then withdrew by the same route.	

(Sgd) W. J. Hilton 2/Lt.
No 5 Platoon.

Patrol Reports for Night 8-3-18.

A. Company.

Patrol Leader. LEGROVE Strength 5 & 1 N.C.O. Hours when out 6.15 - 8.30pm	Orders given to Patrols & by whom	Information obtained Route Taken	Remarks of Patrol Leader Regt of prisoners - enemy patrols met, offensive action taken etc.
	To secure identification by patrolling track and suspected enemy listening post	as per attached sketch plan.	Patrol consisting of 5 men, 1 N.C.O. 1 officer was taken out from point H.11.a.1.0 by the Intelligence Officer and Scout Sergt to point indicated on Sketch. Route of Patrol shewn. Patrol prevented from pushing further forward by water & wire. Remained at extreme end of route for a considerable time as listening post. During this period several Very lights were sent up in our direction from approx position of M.G. emplacement at H.11.d.35.05. No Enemy seen.

Remarks of Commanding Officer.

Copy

8.2.18

SKETCH PLAN SHEWING ROUTE TAKEN BY PATROL.

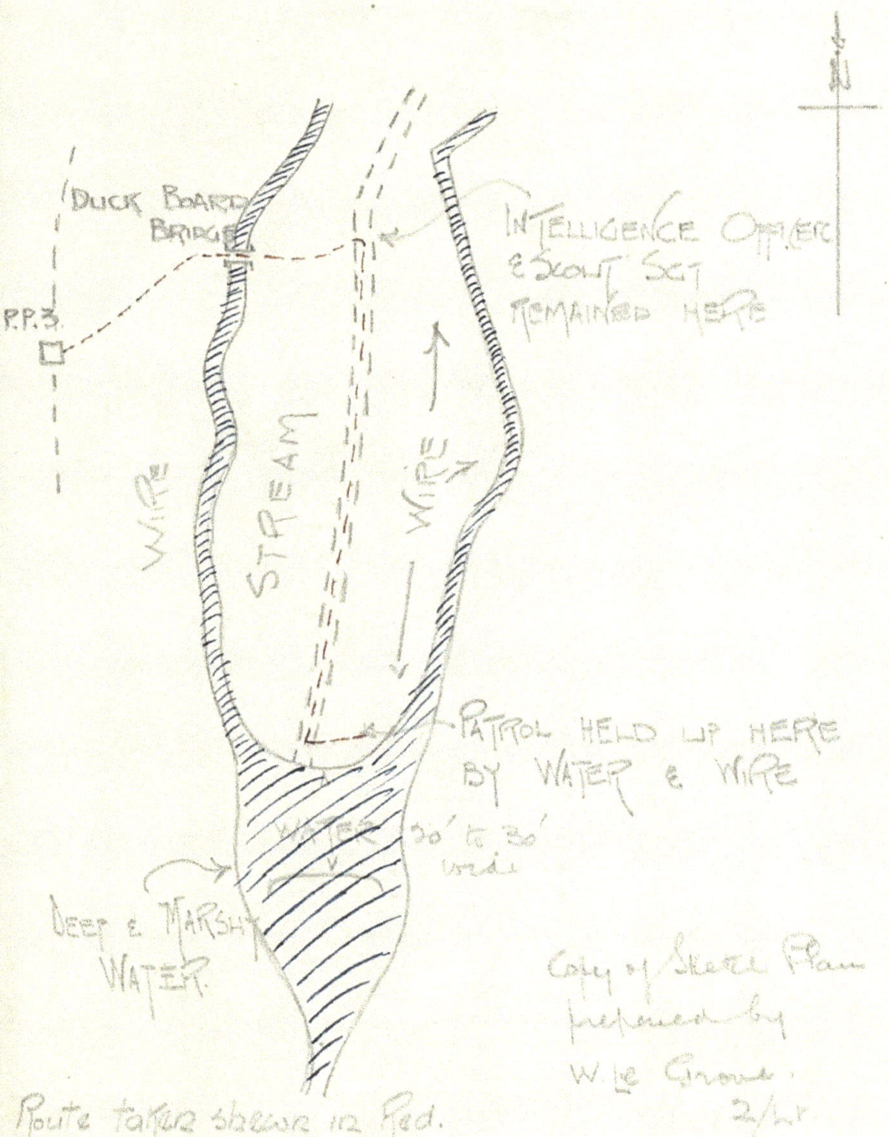

Route taken shewn in Red.
Water Blue.

Copy of Sketch Plan
prepared by
W. Le Grove.
2/Lt
No 1 Platoon.

Patrol Report for Night 8/9 March 1918.

Patrol leader - 2nd/Lt H.B. DARRINGTON Strength. O.R. 5. Hours when out 1am - 3am	Orders given to patrol By whom.	Information obtained Route taken.	Remarks of Patrol Leader.
	To patrol along bank at H.5.d. - H.11.b. to obtain an identification and locate enemy posts	No enemy seen or heard. Patrol moved along road from H.5.d.5.7 to H.5.d.9.4 hence along bank for 150x Movement along bank is difficult owing to noise caused by long dry grass	When patrol moved along the bank three men were left at point H.5.d.9.4. in order to prevent any enemy moving in rear of patrol.

(Signed) H.B. Darrington
2/Lt
'B' Company

PATROL REPORTS FOR NIGHT ..9 March..... 1918.

Patrol leader (Name 247 H.V. ROLLINS Strength O.R. 4 Hours when out. 6 P.M. – 8 P.M.	Orders given to Patrols and by whom.	Information obtained Route taken.	Remarks of Patrol leader (Regt. of prisoners – enemy patrols met, offensive action taken etc)
	To examine wire and ground in front of P.P.1A being a suspected area [illegible] by enemy patrols and to engage any such patrols met for the purpose of [illegible] identification. By O.C. "A" Coy	Wire in front appears to be fairly thick. A small gap was cut through this and the going was good for about 100x. After this the ground became soft and marshy until the patrol was over ankle deep in water and going very heavy. Patrol returned [illegible]	P.P.1A through gap in wire patrol then [illegible] E.S.E. for about [illegible]x then E for 25x, then E.N.E. for another 25x and then [illegible] ground became impassable and had to return. The ground here is almost impassable and the slightest movement causes a great deal of noise. It is highly probable that an enemy patrol could get as far as this. [illegible signature]

A [illegible]

[illegible]

[illegible]

[illegible]

Copy

Patrol Report for Night 10/11 Mai 1918

A Coy

Patrol Leader L. Duckett. Strength O.R. 3. Time when out 6.30pm – 9.30pm	Orders given to patrol & by whom	Information obtained / Route Taken	Remarks of patrol leader (Rept of prisoners, enemy Patrols met, Offensive Action taken etc)
	To reconnoitre vicinity of Chalatte Road & H.17.a.75.90. by O.C. A Coy.	Route taken. H.11.c.10.15. H.11.c.20.15. H.17 a.30.90 H.17a.85.85. Returned same way.	Patrol at outset disturbed waterfowl at H.11.c.3.1 which immediately brought M.G. fire from H.11 d.4.6. Chalatte Road is good going, but there is swamp & abattis on both sides of the road all the way. At H.17.a.3.9. patrol leader discovered a taut cord not cotton stretched across the road. This was most probably a booby trap. No other sign of the enemy was encountered.

(Sgd) Lewis Duckett 2/Lt
i/c Patrol

copy

A

Patrol Report for Night 11/12 March 1918

Patrol Leader (2/Lt Duckett) Strength 2 Offrs 4 OR. Hours when out 7pm - 10 30pm	Orders given to Patrol & by whom	Information obtained & Route taken	
	To reconnoitre wire reported last night on Chalake Road to lay booby trap & await developments with a view to obtaining an identification	Proceeded along Chalake Road to H.17.a.90.80. It was found that the wire had been removed. Patrol then heard a large party of the enemy going in direction of H.17.a.80.90. We withdrew to H.17.a.70.80 & fixed up a booby trap of two Mills bombs, then we withdrew a further 30 yards and listened. Noise of movement & work were heard on the left of the road. At about 10.15 pm our own Artillery opened fire over "No Mans Land" in front of "A" Coy Sector & patrol withdrew. Our booby trap was laid at H.17.a.80.80. It is suspected that there is a Bosche L.P. placed at H.17.a.95.80. Slight sounds were heard there & patrol leader saw a small red light like a cigarette at this place.	

(Sgd) L. Duckett.
2/Lieut
i/c Patrol

SECRET. "The Rangers." Copy No. 17

OPERATION ORDER No. 115.

Reference Sheet 70d, N.W., 1/20,000.

1. "C" Company will relieve "A" Company and "D" Company (less special party) "B" Company in the line to-morrow, 12th March, 1918. One platoon of "A" Company will take the place of the Pioneer Platoon at Bn. H.Q. The remainder of "A" and "B" Companies will take over billets in SINCENY from their opposite Companies. The Pioneer Platoon will be attached to "D" Company, and will take over from the left platoon of "B" Company. O.C., Pioneer Platoon will reconnoitre the position during to-morrow morning.

2. Companies will move by half platoons at 10 minutes interval, the first half platoon of "C" Company passing road junction at G.11.c.90.55. at 10 a.m., first of "D" Company at 2 p.m. Route: Track running through G.11.c. - G.12.c.d. - H.7.c. to point H.7.c.95.85. - thence by track along N. edge of BASSE FORET to point H.9.a.15.45.

3. Lewis Guns and magazines of "C" and "D" Companies, accompanied by Nos. 1 and 2 of each gun will be sent up to-night with the ration column. These guns will take the place of "A" and "B" Companies' guns in the line. As soon as they are in position "A" and "B" Companies' guns will be withdrawn. These together with the magazines and accompanied by Nos. 1 and 2 of each gun will be taken back on the limbers. On arrival at SINCENY the gun numbers will report to the O.C. their opposite Company under whose orders they will remain for the night. O.C., "C" and "D" Companies will arrange for the exchange of magazines, taking care that the gun positions are not denuded during the process.

4. Blankets will remain as trench billet stores and will be duly taken over. Other baggage of "C" and "D" Companies will come up with the ration limbers to-morrow night under arrangements to be made between O.C., Companies and the Transport Officer, and that of "A" and "B" Companies returned by the same means.

5. Completion of relief will be notified to Battalion H.Q. by outgoing Company Commanders in person.

6. ACKNOWLEDGE.

Issued at 3.30 pm

11th March, 1918.

H E Clarke
Lieut. & A/Adjt.,
"The Rangers."

Copy No. 1 Retained.
2 175th Infantry Brigade.
3 10th Londons.
4 8th "
5 9th "
6 Major A.D. Worthington, M.C.
7 O.C., "A" Company.
8 "B"
9 "C"
10 "D"
11 H.Q.
12 The Transport Officer.
13 The Quartermaster.
14 The Medical Officer.
15 R.S.M.
16 } War
17 } Diary.

"THE RANGERS" ORDERLY ROOM. No. 00115 Date 11-3-18. 12th LONDON REGT.

SECRET. "The Rangers." Copy No. 8

OPERATION ORDER No.116.

1. "D" Company special party will relieve No. 4 Platoon, "[illegible]" Company at LA [illegible] to-morrow, 14th instant, about 4 p.m. No. 4 Platoon will return to billets at [illegible] to be arranged by Capt. V.L.BURNSIDE. One N.C.O. will report to Capt. BURNSIDE at 11 a.m. Route as in Operation Order No 115

2. Rations for the special party will be sent up with H.Q. Company rations to-morrow night.
Baggage will come up with the rations under arrangements to be made by Capt. L.K.SPENCER direct with the Transport Officer.
Blankets will be handed over as trench and billet stores.

3. Completion of relief will be reported to Battalion H.Q. by the N.C.O. in charge No. 4 platoon in person.

Issued at 11.30 pm

13th March, 1918.

H E Ebbutt
Lieut. & A/Adjt.,
"The Rangers."

Copy No. 1 Retained.
2 Capt. L.K.SPENCER.
3 Capt. V.L.BURNSIDE.
4 N.C.O. i/c No. 4 platoon.
5 The Quartermaster.
6 The Transport Officer.
7 R.S.M.
8 War Diary.

Patrol Report for Night 13/14 March 1918.

Patrol Leader (Name) L.K. Spencer. Strength O.R. 6. Hours when out 9.30 pm – 12.25 am	Orders given to patrols and by whom	Information obtained Route taken	Remarks of Patrol Leader (Regt of prisoners, enemy patrols met, offensive action taken etc.)
	Object of patrol ① To reconnoitre bank running from OLD MILL – BRIQUENAY FARM Road southwards (from H. 5.d. 8.3 to COPSE at H.11. b. 8.6.) ② To obtain identification if any enemy patrols were met ③ To examine wire north of copse. — L.K. Spencer (Capt)	① Route from P.P.6 to road at H.5.d.5.7 thence to bank at H5.d.8.3 thence along east side of bank about 25 yds from it. ② The going is quite good & if fallen trees are avoided a patrol or raiding party can proceed quietly. The bank itself is not quickly accessible for cover owing to numerous fallen trees which appear to have been felled at the bank towards the enemy lines. Ground rises steeply from bank for a distance eastwards of about 50 yards. A party walking 30 yds to the east of & parallel to bank could not be seen from the Bosche wire. No path was discovered in the wire which broadens as one proceeds southwards and where it is broadest it is also thickest. Limit southwards which patrol reached was H 11. b. 80.75. ③ A T.M. fired on P.P.4 while patrol was at H.11. b. 90.95. It appeared to have been fired from about H.12 a. 10.50.	

(Sgd) L.K. Spencer Capt.
OC. D Coy
"Rangers"

2/Lt K.H.S. Clarke.
2/Lt W.G. Wood.
14.

9.30pm - 1am

(1) To reconnoitre route to copse at H.11.b central from H.11.a.6.5. (2) To detach a party from patrol on reaching Copse to the end of the wire belt which appears to exist at H.11.b.7.7 (100 yds N.E. of copse) to report on this gap & rejoin patrol (3) To move on S side of copse towards H.11.b.95.50 to ascertain amount & location of Bosche wire	Route. Exit from our line over Bridge at H.11.a Central to a distance of 200x E of it.	The route is very noisy obstructed by many bands of French wire & tabattes. About 30x W of the second stream at H.11.a.6.5 an enemy patrol (estimated at about 3) was encountered and fired on by the patrol. Enemy patrol replied with fire. While firing further movement was heard to the S of the patrol & one of the enemy patrol fell as if hit. Orders were given to cease fire & 3 men of our patrol moved forward to investigate. To do this more wire was encountered & on reaching the place from which the yell appeared to come a search was made without result. Patrol heard movement at various points in front & 2/Lt Wood returned to our lines with 1 O.R. to obtain more ammunition. The patrol again moved forward & each advance made drew fire from an enemy M.G.

P.T.O.

It appeared as if the M.G was firing from the bank at H.11.a.8.5 from which the noise of movement near the Second Stream could be heard by enemy at that point.

After many attempts to go forward & each attempt being met by enemy M.G fire patrol was withdrawn to our lines at 1 a.m.

Patrol Report for night 15/16th March 1918

Copy

Patrol leader, Strength O.R., Hours when out	Orders given to patrol & by whom	Information obtained & route taken	Remarks of Patrol leader
Capt. L.K. Spencer 15 O.R. 8 pm – 10.7 pm	(1) Patrol to consist of (a) main body & of: (b) a covering party (a) 1 off. + 10 O.R. (b) 1 Sgt + 4 O.R. Duty of covering party to precede the advance & establish themselves at the point A & remain until patrol [illegible] Duty of main party to reconnoitre route to pt. B to see if there is a gap there & if there is a then to a gap to proceed as near as possible to the wood to the west	Route shown by red line on attached map From PP6 – A – B – C C is 30 yds from front or west edge of CLOS LENTHORN wood.	The advance through own wire from PP6 towards the road at OLD MILL was [illegible] [illegible] by cutting a pathway through the [illegible]. Patrol was able to move out to the road in 11 minutes. The covering party preceded main party by 7 [illegible]. The [illegible] [illegible] [illegible] & [illegible] until main party formed S of point A [illegible] [illegible] [illegible] rustles when walked upon. Before reaching point B [illegible] [illegible] [illegible] the bank [illegible] [illegible] [illegible] [illegible] [illegible] back. There can be [illegible] [illegible] [illegible] immediately beyond these two [illegible] [illegible] of 15 yds in the [illegible] [illegible] [illegible] [illegible] being [illegible] E & W. On each of the [illegible] of these [illegible] [illegible] ship [illegible] placed & at a point [illegible] [illegible] was a white handkerchief [illegible] [illegible] [illegible] [illegible] found [illegible] should be possible [illegible] [illegible] The extent [illegible]

further advance

The wire as previously reported is extraordinarily thick & consists of small pickets with barb wire and a large quantity of loose thick wire. None of it at this point was higher than 3 ft.

From this point 1 officer & 3 OR advanced towards the wood which was very quiet. After two halts to listen this party reached a point (C on attached map) 30 yds from the edge of the wood.

The wood held by the enemy was remarkably quiet & very little sound of [illegible] was heard except an occasional cough of a man well within the wood, neither was any sound heard from the Copse on the right of patrol.

Patrol returned in half an hour at [illegible] [illegible] A. R. Spencer Capt

[illegible]

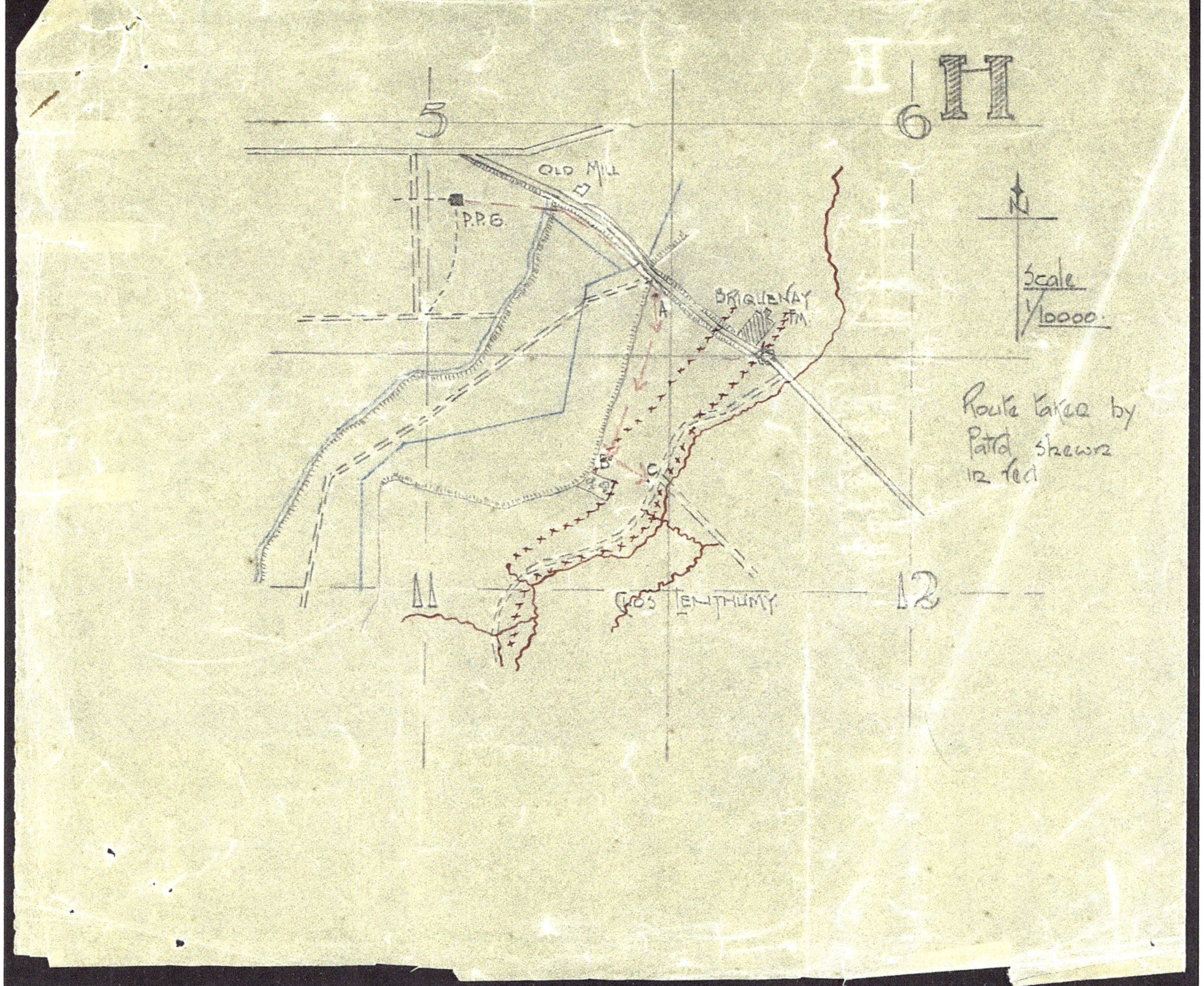

H
5
6
11
12
OLD MILL
P.P.G.
A
B
C
BRIQUENAY FM.
CLOS LENTHUMY
N
Scale 1/10000.
Route taken by Patrol shewn in red

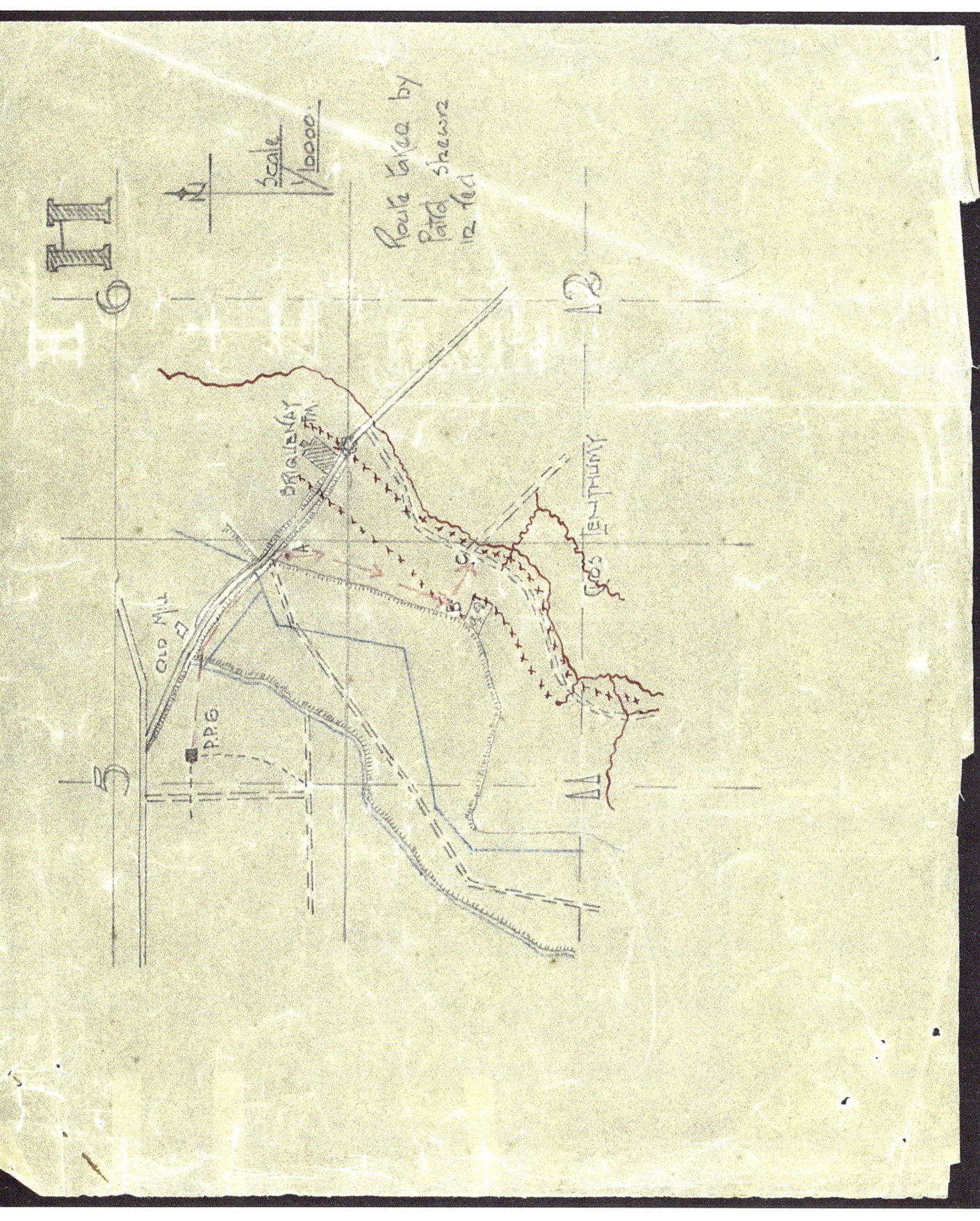

SECRET. "The Rangers." Copy No. 17

OPERATION ORDER No. 110.

Reference Sheet 70d, N.W., 1/20,000.

1. "A" Company will relieve "C" Company and "B" Company "D" Company in the line to-day, 17th March, 1918. "D" Company Special Party will be withdrawn to LA FORTELLE and will occupy billets lately vacated by the Q.V.Rs.
"C" Company and the remainder of "D" Company will take over billets in SINCENY from their opposite Companies. The Pioneer Platoon will return to their original quarters at LA FORTELLE after relief.

2. Companies will move by half platoons at 10 minutes interval, the first half platoon of "A" Company passing road junction at G.11.a. 90.85. at 4 p.m.; the first of "B" Company at 6 p.m. Route: track running through G.11.c. - G.12.c.d. - H.7.c. to point H.7.c.95.85. - thence by track along N. edge of BASSE FORET to point H.9.b.15.45.

3. Lewis Guns, accompanied by Nos. 1 and 2 of each gun, will come up with the ration column. "C" and "D" Companies guns will be taken back on these limbers after being relieved.

4. Blankets will remain as trench and billet stores. Other baggage of "A" and "B" Companies will come up with the ration limbers under arrangements to be made between O.C., Companies and the Transport Officer, and that of "C" and "D" Companies returned by the same means. Field Cookers will come up at the same time.

5. Completion of relief will be notified ~~xxxxxxxx~~ to Battalion H.Q. by outgoing Company Commanders in person.

6. ACKNOWLEDGE.

Issued at 9 am

17th March, 1918.

H E Blenkin
Lieut. & A/Adjt.,
"The Rangers."

Copy No. 1 Retained.
2 175th Infantry Brigade.
3 10th Londons.
4 8th "
5 9th "
6 Major W.G. Worthington, M.C.
7 O.C., "A" Company.
8 "B"
9 "C"
10 "D"
11 H.Q.
12 The Transport Officer.
13 The Quartermaster.
14 The Medical Officer.
15 O.C., Pioneer Platoon.
16 R.S.M.
17 } War
18 } Diary.

SECRET. "The Rangers." Copy No. 11

OPERATION ORDER, No. 117.

Reference Sheet 70d. 1/20,000.

1. From midnight 18/19th March the front of the Brigade will be held by one Battalion, and the Village Line - LA FORTELLE KEEP - [illegible] KEEP - APPLE KEEP, including the area held by the support companies of the left Battalion, will form the front line of the Battle Zone.

2. The Rangers will be relieved in the Forward Zone by the Q.V.Rs.
"A" Coy. Rangers being relieved by "[illegible]" Coy, Q.V.R.
"B" " " " " "B" " "
Platoon guides from "A" and "B" Coy., Rangers, will report to Orderly Room at 7.30 a.m. to-morrow to proceed to the BUTTES to guide Q.V.R. Companies into the line.
"[illegible]" Coy., Q.V.R. may be expected about 9.[illegible] a.m. and "[illegible]" Coy., Q.V.R. about an hour later.

3. On relief "A" Company, Rangers, will take over LA FORTELLE KEEP from Bn. H.Q. with two platoons and Company H.Q., and the two forward posts of "[illegible]" Company, Q.V.R. with one platoon each. Guides from these two posts will meet representatives of "A" Coy., Rangers at Bn. H.Q. at 8.30 a.m. to show position of Posts just in rear of LA FORTELLE KEEP. "A" Company, Rangers, will only take over trench stores for the two forward posts from "[illegible]" Company, Q.V.R. An N.C.O. to take these over and trench stores at LA FORTELLE KEEP will report at Bn. H.Q. at 8.30 a.m.
On relief "B" Coy, Rangers, will occupy the position vacated by "B" Coy., Q.V.R. at the RIGHT BUTTS, becoming reserve company for the Battle Zone. "B" Coy. Rangers, will send an Officer and N.C.O. to take over the dugout ([illegible] approximately) to be at the BUTTES at 10 a.m. This Officer and N.C.O. will act as guide for guiding the Company into position.
After relief "A" and "B" Coys will come under the orders of O.C. 2/10th Bn. London Regiment.

4. On relief Battalion H.Q. will move back to billets at SINCENY.

5. C.S.Ms and Signals from Q.V.R. will arrive at Coy. H.Q. at 7.15 a.m. to take over stores, etc.,

6. Lewis Guns and magazines will be carried by Companies. "A" Coy. will also carry their blankets. "B" Company and H.Q. will dump their blankets and baggage at Coy and Bn. H.Q., respectively.
The Transport Officer will arrange enough transport to move "B" Coys. Lewis Guns and magazines and the baggage of "B" Coy. and H.Q. to the BUTTES and SINCENY respectively.

7. The Transport Officer will arrange to withdraw "A" Company's Field Cooker to LA FORTELLE and "B" Company's to the BUTTES. In the case of the latter cooking utensils will then be off-loaded and the cooker returned to the Transport lines.
The Water Cart at present at LA FORTELLE will be withdrawn to the BUTTES.

Issued at 6pm

17th March, 1918.

H E Blake

Lieut. & A/Adjt.,
"The Rangers."

DISTRIBUTION.

Copy No. 1 Retained.
2 175th Infantry Brigade.
3 O.C., 8th Londons
4 9th
5 10th
6 Major [illegible], R.E.
7 O.C., "A" Company.
8 "B"
9 "C"
10 "D"
11 H.Q.
12 The Transport Officer.
13 The Quartermaster.
14 The Medical Officer.
15 R.S.M.
16) War
17) Diary.

SECRET. "The Rangers." Copy No. 13.

OPERATION ORDER No. 118.

Reference Sheet, 70d, 1/20,000.

1. The Rangers H.Q. and "C" and "D" Companies will move into positions as under to-day:-
H.Q. - LA FORTELLE KEEP. "C" Coy. - LA FORTELLE KEEP. "D" Coy - BUTTES, Right Locality.
Order of march: as above by half platoons at five minutes interval.
First half-platoon of H.Q. to pass cross roads at G.17.b.90.10. at 4 p.m. 15 minutes interval between Companies.
Route: By track running along N. edge of [illegible].

2. Lewis Guns of "C" and "D" Coys. and 20 magazines per gun will be carried on pack ponies, 2 of which will report at each Company H.Q. at 4.30 p.m.
Blankets and baggage of H.Q. and "C" and "D" Companies and the remainder of the Lewis Gun magazines will be dumped at Bn. and Company H.Q. and will be taken up by the Transport to-night.

3. The Transport Officer will arrange to take up the field cookers of all Companies. Also one water cart at LA FORTELLE.

4. When Companies are in position the Company Commander's surname will be wired to H.Q.

Issued at ________

Lieut. & A/Adjt.,
"The Rangers."

19th March, 1918.

DISTRIBUTION.

Copy No. 1 Retained.
2 178th Infantry Brigade.
3 Major [illegible].G. Worthington, M.C.
4 O.C., "A" Company.
5 "B"
6 "C"
7 "D"
8 H.Q.
9 The Transport Officer.
10 The Quartermaster.
11 The Medical Officers.
12 R.S.M.
13) War
14) Diary.

WOUNDED SLIGHTLY AT DUTY:

G/1851	Pte	Banfield G.	21/3/18
949	"	Kemp W.	21/3/18
G/1787	"	Price L S.	21/3/18
G/5720	"	Freeman W H.	21/3/18
G/2605	"	Short W.	22/3/18
20068	"	Ridgway W.	22/3/18
G/1847	"	Bailey H G.	24/3/18
G/8589	L/Cpl	Gardner F.	24/3/18
291235	Pte	Loon A.	24/3/18
G/2236	"	Cheeseman G.	24/3/18
G/2587	"	Trigwell A.	24/3/18
G/2023	"	Whiter B A.	28/3/18

****

175th Inf.Bde.
58th Div.

WAR DIARY

12th BATTN. THE LONDON REGIMENT.
(THE RANGERS)

A P R I L

1 9 1 8

Attached:

Appendices.

17

175/58 Vol 16

War Diary

The Rangers 12 / Lond

Volume Two

April 1916

Instructions regarding War Diaries and Intelligence Summaries are contained in F. S. Regs., Part II. and the Staff Manual respectively. Title pages will be prepared in manuscript.

WAR DIARY
or
INTELLIGENCE SUMMARY.
(Erase heading not required.)

Army Form C. 2118.

Place	Date	Hour	Summary of Events and Information	Remarks and references to Appendices
ABBECOURT SECTOR	1-4-18		On completion of relief HQ + 2 platoons of "A" Coy take over garrison of strong point at BAC d'ABLINCOURT	
		1·20 AM	Reported to Brigade - Situation quiet -	
		2 PM	Warning Order for Relief by French received -	
		4 PM	Dump on fire observed at ABBECOURT	
		4·30 "	French Officer arrived to arrange for taking over Front Line W of OISE & AISNE CANAL	
			Reported to Brigade - Situation quiet -	
		7 30 "	-do- -do-	
	2·4·18	6 AM	Reported to Brigade - Situation quiet -	
		4 PM	-ditto-	
		7 PM	-ditto-	
			French Infantry take over Battalion Front on E of OISE & AISNE CANAL and also on WEST.	
			O.C "RANGERS" to remain at present HQ in command of old BN SECTOR until 8 AM 3-4-18.	
		11 PM	O.C. "B" Coy report relief complete	
		11·20 "	O.C "D" Coy report RIVER OISE rising rapidly + that all forward posts had been withdrawn except that at L.17 a.7.7 with approval of French relieving Officer - Reported information to 174 Inf. Bde + instructed OC "D" Coy to order French Officer to report to his C.O. + to the troops on his right - Ordered LIAISON OFFICER at BN HQ to report to FRENCH Unit on our left.	OO 121 att.
		11·50	O.C. Right Forward Coy. reported that the FORWARD POSTS are still out on the left of the CANAL but that the river is rising there, but not to the same extent	
		12 MID.	Relief complete and reported to BDE	
	3-4-18		On relief Companies marched to ST PAUL AUX BOIS, accommodated in large French huts.	
		8 AM	Command of Battn Sector astride OISE & AISNE CANAL passed to the FRENCH -	
			OC "RANGERS" at BAC d'ABLINCOURT reaching ST PAUL AUX BOIS about 9 am	
ST PAUL AUX BOIS			a few shells fell round the village during the day - NO casualties -	
		6·45 PM	Battalion proceeded by march route to ANDIGNICOURT - Order of march "HQ", "A", "B" "C" + "D" Coys Route through BLERENCOURT	OO 122 att
ANDIGNICOURT		11 PM	Bn in billets	

D. D. & L., London, E.C.
(A8004) Wt. W1771/M2·31 750,000 5/17 Sch. 52 Forms/C2118/14

Instructions regarding War Diaries and Intelligence Summaries are contained in F. S. Regs., Part II. and the Staff Manual respectively. Title pages will be prepared in manuscript.

WAR DIARY
or
INTELLIGENCE SUMMARY.
(Erase heading not required.)

Army Form C. 2118.

Place	Date	Hour	Summary of Events and Information	Remarks and references to Appendices
ANDIGNICOURT	4-4-18	10.40 AM	Battalion moved by march route to billets at LAVERSINE – Order of march HQ, A, B, C & D Coys – Route VIC-SUR-AISNE, COEUVRE.	OO 123 att.
LAVERSINE		4.30 PM	Reached LAVERSINE	
	5-4-18		Bn proceeded to VILLERS-COTTERETS for entrainment	OO.124 att.
		6 AM	"A" Coy proceeded to VILLERS-COTTERETS as BRIGADE loading party –	
		1.10 PM	Transport left for VILLERS-COTTERETS	
		2.40 "	Battalion proceeded by march route for VILLERS-COTTERETS – Order of march HQ, B, C & D Coys	
VILLERS-COTTERETS		6.30 "	Reached VILLERS-COTTERETS Station	
		8 PM	Battalion entrained –	
LONGEAU	6.4.18		Battalion reached LONGEAU and detrained –	
			Battalion proceeded by march route to WOOD, 2500 yds NE of BOVES	
		2 PM	Battalion left WOOD for RESERVE ~~LINE~~ POSITION exclusive of AMIENS-ROUY road and inclusive of GENTELLES (T.24.b. to U.7.c. Sheet 62d. 1/40000) Bn HQ S of BOIS de GENTELLES in T.17.c	
			Relieved AUSTRALIAN Infantry –	
		6.30 PM	Relief complete	
			Situation quiet on Bn Front.	
BOIS de GENTELLES	7.4.18		Situation quiet on Bn Front –	
			Preparations made for wiring whole Bn Front with double apron entanglements tonight –	
		3 PM	Orders received to take over LEFT of Front Line from 5TH AUSTRALIAN BDE – SE of VILLERS-BRETONNEUX, tonight	
		3.45 "	Conference of CO's with Brigade Major at 5TH AUSTRALIAN BDE HQ, GENTELLES –	
VILLERS-BRETONNEUX		8.30 "	Bn left position for Front Line – Relieved 17TH AUSTRALIAN INF. BN	OO 125 att.
			Distribution "B", "C" + "D" Coys right to left in Front Line – "A" Coy in Support – Bn HQ in VILLERS-BRETONNEUX.	
	8-4-18	2 AM	Relief complete	
		4 AM	Reported to Brigade – Situation quiet generally – Slight hostile shelling of VILLERS-BRETONNEUX	
		4 PM	Reported to Brigade situation quiet – casualties NIL	

D. D. & L., London, E.C.
(A8004) Wt. W1771/M2 31 750,000 5/17 Sch. 52 Forms/C2118/14

Army Form C. 2118.

Instructions regarding War Diaries and Intelligence Summaries are contained in F. S. Regs., Part II. and the Staff Manual respectively. Title pages will be prepared in manuscript.

WAR DIARY
or
INTELLIGENCE SUMMARY.
(Erase heading not required.)

Place	Date	Hour	Summary of Events and Information	Remarks and references to Appendices
VILLERS-BRETONNEUX	9-4-18	4.30 AM 5.0 "	Concentrated shelling of front edge of village and shelling of back areas.	
		6.0 " 6.25 "	Shelling repeated but nearer support line	
		7.15 "	Received warning order that the 9th LONDON REGT would be relieved by 2/10th LONDON REGT tonight.	
		9.0 "	Shelling round Battalion HQ.	
		9.25 "	Quieter –	
		11.30 "	2 Officers of 35th AUSTRALIAN INF. called and were given dispositions –	
		12.15 PM	Shelling of bridge near Bn HQ recommenced	
		12.55 "	Reported to Brigade Major that shelling was from a 4.2" ringing from approx 124 true bearing from here (MARCELCAVE)	
	10-4-18	2.30 AM	C.S.M "B" Coy rang up that OC "B" Coy very ill.	
		2.40 "	2nd Lt. WILLIAMS R.J. proceeded to join "B" Coy –	
		2.42 "	Guns firing short on "B" Coy Front.	
		2.43 "	Liaison Officer dealt with above.	
		2.44 "	2/Lt GORSUCH H. rang up to say that O.C "B" Coy & another officer very ill –	
		3.30 "	P.T. reports –	
		4.0 "	2nd/Lt R.J WILLIAMS reported arrival at "B" Coy HQ. & that invalids had been sent to AID POST	
		4.30 "	O.C. "B" Coy & 2/Lt H.B. DARRINGTON arrived from Aid Post & sent to bed – complaint – COLIC –	
		5.30 "	Daylight – All quiet on front –	
		6.0 "	Our aeroplanes very active –	
		9.30 "	About 27 of our aeroplanes over front	
		10.0 "	O.C "K" Battery R.H.A visited us for news – battery situated N of RLY in O.27.d.	
		10.10 "	2 of our 'planes reported by Right Front Coy to have fired on our trenches – Reported to Brigade –	
		10.15 "	French 'plane hit but landed under control in our lines –	
		4 PM	Reported to Brigade – Situation quiet –	
	11-4-18	5.30 AM	Concentrated Artillery fire heard some distance away on our right.	
		6.15 "	All quiet on our sector –	
		9.15 "	Renewed shelling of area near cross roads about O.35.b.8.4. – Rate 2 shells per minutes.	
		11.55 "	Renewed shelling as above – Rate of fire 5 per minute –	
		12.10 "	Range lengthened slightly – Shelling continued at slower rate –	

Instructions regarding War Diaries and Intelligence Summaries are contained in F. S. Regs., Part II. and the Staff Manual respectively. Title pages will be prepared in manuscript.

WAR DIARY
or
INTELLIGENCE SUMMARY.
(Erase heading not required.)

Army Form C. 2118.

Place	Date	Hour	Summary of Events and Information	Remarks and references to Appendices
VILLERS-BRETONNEUX	11-4-18	4.44 PM	Large enemy convoy observed by our LEFT Front Coy - to be moving from P.36.c.8.5. towards LAMOTTE EN SANTERRE	
		4.55 "	Informed Brigade -	
		5.15 "	Left Front Coy reports being heavily shelled + may have to vacate present Coy HQ.	
	12-4-18		Patrols sent out -	2 Reports attached }
			Enemy artillery not very active during day or night upon our front line -	
		1.45 AM	Village shelled with 4.2s at rate of 5 per minute for 5 minutes and 2 per minute for 10 minutes from MARCELCAVE	
		8.30 PM	"A" Coy relieved "B" Coy on right of Front line	
			2/Lt C W SEED - wounded + evacuated -	
			MAJOR W.G. WORTHINGTON M.C. Wounded (and at duty) in back areas. (AMIENS)	
			8 Officers + 85 O.R. Battle Surplus proceeded to LONGPRE to joint DIV Battle Surplus - Major W.G. WORTHINGTON MC did not proceed with party -	
	13-4-18		Patrols sent out -	2 Reports att.
			Very little enemy artillery activity - Our guns fired practice barrage -	
		9 PM	Battalion relieved by 6TH LONDON REGT + proceeded to Reserve position vacated by 7TH LONDON REGT in BLANGY WOOD	OO 126 att.
BLANGY WOOD			32 reinforcements arrived from Depot Battalion -	
	14-4-18	2 AM	Garrisoned at Railway Cutting N of BLANGY WOOD and remained there until dawn when we moved into positions in the wood as Battalion in Brigade Reserve	
			Major W G WORTHINGTON MC proceeded to join Battle Surplus with 5 O R.	
	15-4-18		Battalion rested	OO. 127 att.
		6.30 PM	Battalion relieved by 36th AUSTRALIAN INF.	
		9 PM	Battalion arrived in billets at GLISY	
GLISY	16-4-18		Battalion rested, refitted and bathed -	
	17-4-18		- ditto - Recent drafts inspected by C O + Brigadier General -	
	18-4-18		Battalion rested, refitted and bathed	
		1 PM	Major W.G. WORTHINGTON MC reported from 3rd Corps Reinforcement Camp to relieve C O who departed on leave -	
		6.30 "	Battalion moved into Reserve trenches S of GENTELLES WOOD.	

D. D. & L., London, E.C.
(A8004) Wt. W1771/M2031 750,000 5/17 Sch. 52 Forms/C2118/14

Army Form C. 2118.

Instructions regarding War Diaries and Intelligence Summaries are contained in F. S. Regs., Part II. and the Staff Manual respectively. Title pages will be prepared in manuscript.

WAR DIARY
or
INTELLIGENCE SUMMARY.
(Erase heading not required.)

Place	Date	Hour	Summary of Events and Information	Remarks and references to Appendices
GENTELLES WOOD	19-4-18 to 20-4-18		Bn occupied reserve position at S.E. of BOIS de GENTELLES	
	20-4-18	9 pm	Battalion relieved 2/10th London Regt at Reserve Line SE. of Bois de GENTELLES. Battalion HQ remained at SE Corner of BOIS de GENTELLES.	
	21-4-18		Battalion engaged upon improving defences of CACHY SWITCH	
	22-4-18		Gas shells fell at Bn HQ causing heavy casualties amongst HQ Officers & other ranks which were as follows:- Major W.G. WORTHINGTON MC; 2Lt (A/Capt) DEB COPELAND (Adjt); Lieut DH STONES; 2/Lt WE WOOD; 2/Lt RJ WILLIAMS + 36 other ranks. Capt VL BURNSIDE commanding "A" Coy was withdrawn to Bn HQ to command Battalion. 2/Lt SG BEER MC was brought up from Transport Lines as A/Adjutant	
	23-4-18		Area at GENTELLES and the BOIS de GENTELLES was heavily shelled by Gas Shells. No casualties in the Battalion.	
	24-4-18 to 30-4-18		A summary of operations between these dates is in course of preparation, but cannot be attached at present until all details are completed	

W.K. Spencer Capt & Adjt
for
Major
Comdg "The Rangers" 12th London Regt

D. D. & L., London, E.C.
(A8004) Wt. W1771/M2731 750,000 5/17 Sch. 52 Forms/C2118/14

A P P E N D I C E S .

Secret. "The Rangers" Copy No. 1

Operation Order 121

Ref: Sheets 70d and 70e. 1/40,000

1. On the night of 2/3rd April the Bn. will be relieved as under:-

D Coy. plus 2 platoon A Coy by one Coy 363 French Regiment.

B " (and one Coy. Fusilier Bn) by 3 Coys 4th Bn. 246 French Regiment

C " and 2 Coys. 18th Ent. Bn. and 2 Coys. Fusilier Bn by 2 Coys 6th Bn. 246 French Regt.

2. When French dispositions are reported complete Coys. will withdraw to ST. PAUL AUX BOIS to billets being taken over by CQMSs to-day.

An Officer from Bn. H.Q. will be at bridge M.1.b.00.70. to check platoons as they pass.

Bn. H.Q. party and "A" Coy H.Q. and 2 platoons will move on receipt of orders from Bn. H.Q. On arrival at ST. PAUL AUX BOIS O.C. "A" Coy. will take over his 2 platoons at present attached to "D" Coy.

3. Liaison. (a) One Officer to be detailed by O.C. B Coy. will report at H.Q. 4th Bn. 246th French Regt. at MANICAMP Cross roads L.27.a.7.2. at 7 p.m. today.

(b) One Officer to be detailed by O.C. "C" Coy will report to H.Q. 6th Bn. 246th French Regt 500 yards S. of MANICAMP Cross roads L.27.a.7.2. at 7 p.m. to-day.

These Officers will ascertain when French dispositions are complete and will inform their respective Coys. to this effect and that withdrawal may take place.

(c) One Officer and 2 Signallers (linesmen) to be detailed by O.C. "D" Coy. will report to — Battalion, 363rd French Regiment.

The above personnel will remain with H.Q. French Bns. for 24 hours after completion of relief and will then proceed by lorry. Rendezvous will be notified later.

4. The Transport Officer will arrange for one limber per Coy. to report at Coy. H.Q. as soon as possible after dark to carry L.Gs dixies, etc. "A" Coys limber will report at D Coy. H.Q. and afterwards at Bn. H.Q. for Coy. H.Q. and 2 platoons. These limbers will follow in rear of their respective Coys.

The Transport Officer will also arrange to clear the reserve L.G. magazines and tools now at "C" Coy H.Q. also L.Gs and dixies of H.Q. Coy. The Mess Cart and Maltese Cart will report at Bn. H.Q.

Officers mounts will report with the limbers. Field Cookers and rations for tomorrow will be at ST. PAUL

AUX BOIS
5. The Commanding Officer, Adjutant and Bn. Intelligence Officer, together with personnel as detailed will remain at present Bn H.Q. until 8 a.m. 3rd April when command of the Subsector passes to the French.
6. Completion of relief will be notified to Bn. H.Q. by runner.
7. Acknowledge.

H.E.Blake
Lieut & A/Adjt.
"The Rangers"

Issued at 2 pm
2-4-1918.

Copy No. 1 Retained
2 O.C. A Co.
3 B
4 C
5 D
6 H.Q.
7 M.O.
8 T.O.
9 Q.M.
10 R.S.M.

<u>Secret</u> <u>"The Rangers"</u> <u>Copy No. 7</u>

<u>Operation Order ~~[illegible]~~ 122.</u>

<u>Reference Sheet 70e, 1/40,000.</u>

1. The Bn. will move by march route this evening to ANDIGNICOURT.

2. Movement will be by platoons at 200 yards interval in the following order:- H.Q., A, B, C, D. The first platoon of H.Q. will pass the starting point - junction of road and track R.23.a.9.3 at 6.45 pm. Route:- BLEFANCOURT - Cross roads W.12.b.6.8. - ANDIGNICOURT. No movement will take place until the order "carry on" is sent from H.Q.

3. Lewis Gun limbers & field cookers will follow in rear of their respective Coy. The Mess cart and Maltese cart will follow in rear of H.Q. Coy.

4. On arrival in new area first line transport (except Lewis Gun limbers & field cookers) and baggage wagons will be brigaded in the valley, W.23.b. under arrangements which have already been made.

Issued at
3-4-1918.

[signature]
Lieut & A/Adjt.
"The Rangers"

Copy No. 1 Retained No. 6 OC H.Q.
2 OC A Coy 7 T.O.
3 B 8 Q.M.
4 C 9 M.O.
5 D 10 R.S.M.

SECRET The Rangers Copy 1

Operation Order No 12-3.

1/ The Bn will continue the march tomorrow halting for the night 4th/5th April at COUTRY.

2/ Order of march - HQ - A - B - C - D.
HQ will pass the Starting Point - road junction approx 1/4 mile N.W. of VASSENS village at 10.15 am

3/ Lewis Gun limbers & Field Cookers will march in rear of their respective coys. Remainder of Transport will march in rear of Bn column.

4/ Distances of 500 yds will be maintained between Coys on the march & between the Bn & the Transport.

5/ The usual 10 minutes halts will be observed.
In addition there will be a halt for dinner between 10.50 am & 12 noon

6/ Billeting party of CQMS & one N.C.O. per Coy will report to Major Worthington at Bn HQ at 8.30 am ready to proceed

7. The attention of Company officers is directed to Bn Standing Orders with reference to March Discipline & Transport.
Men carrying packs will as far as possible march together in rear of their respective platoons.
Words of command will always be given by the commander of a Company or Platoon as the case may be whatever his position in the column.

H E Blake

Lieut. & A/Adjutant
The Rangers.

Issued at 12.30 am
4/4/18

Copy No 1 Retained
2 Maj. W.G. Worthington Cmdg.
3 OC A Coy
4 B
5 C
6 D
7 HQ
8 T.O
9 QM
10 RSM

SECRET. "The Rangers." Copy No. 13

OPERATION ORDER No. ~~125.~~ 124

Reference Sketch map attached.

1. The Battalion will entrain at VILLERS COTTERETS to-day.

2. Order of march:- H.Q., "B" "C" "D". H.Q. will pass the starting point - junction of roads from CUTRY and LAVERSINE to COEUVRES - at 2.40 p.m. Route as shown on attached map. Distances of 100 yards will be maintained between Companies.

3. The Transport will pass the starting point at 1.10 p.m. Cookers and L.G. limbers must be ready for yoking up by 12.30 p.m. Water carts will be entrained full.

4. Officers' valises will be at the Quartermasters Stores by 11.30 a.m.

5. Watches to be sent to Battalion H.Q. at 12 noon to be synchronised.

6. ACKNOWLEDGE.

H.E. Clarke

Lieut. & A/Adjt.,
"The Rangers."

Issued at 10 a.m.

5th April, 1918.

Copy No. 1 Retained.
2 175th Infantry Brigade.
3 Major W.G.Worthington, M.C.
4 O.C., "A" Company.
5 "B"
6 "C"
7 "D"
8 H.Q.
9 The Transport Officer.
10 The Quartermaster.
11 The Medical Officer.
12 R.S.M.
13) War
14) Diary.

The Rangers

Operation Order No 127.

Ref. Sheet 62d 1/40000.

1 The Bn will relieve 17th Bn. A.I. tonight in the Front Line from V1b47 to P26d03, distributed as follow

Front Line - Right to Left.

B, C + D Coys each with 3 platoons in front line + 1 platoon in Support.

A Coy will be in Bn Reserve

Bn HQ will be in VILLERS BRETONNEUX at O35b91.

2 Coys will move in following order by [p]latoons at 50 yards

interval – B – C – D – A – H.Q.
Leading platoon will pass
road junction at ~~[illegible]~~ at
U7a80
8.30 pm.
Route CACHY – road junction
O27d24 – railway bridge
O28d14 where guides will
be met.

3/ Company Commanders will
proceed ahead of their Coys
to reconnoitre. Guides
will meet them at O35a71
at 7.30 pm.

4/ All Tools will be carried
forward by Coys.

5/ Transport will move under
direct orders from Bde will

be met by guides at O28a14,
at 12.30am 8th April.

6. Coys will take one spare bandolier of SAA per man where possible & after taking over the line will report to Bn HQ. their requirements in respect of SAA & Bombs & Rocket Signals.

7. Lewis Guns will be carried forward by Coys.

8. Bn Aid Post will be in VILLERS BRETONNEAUX. Exact location later.

9. Relief will be notified to Bn HQ by sending by Company name.

HE Clarke

7/3/18. Lieut A/Adjt

C Coy

Patrol Report

Patrol Leader [illegible] Strength O.R. 4 Time when out	Object with which patrol sent & by whom	Information obtained	Patrol leader's remarks
/	Top end No Mans Land on the left of sector to get identification if possible Capt X B Bell	After leaving road at P.21.d.8.4 went half left for 300x no sign of enemy [illegible] was seen. I was unable to move more than another 40x as Very Lights were sent up and MG opened fire on us. I then went over to the right of road where the same thing occurred	The command of No Mans Land rests entirely in the hands of those with the most MGs & very lights as it is impossible to get very close to enemy posts owing to so many lights going up and MG firing at [illegible]

(Sgd) W T Williams
2/Lt

12-4-18

War Diary   Patrol Report

Patrol Leader (Name) Strength O.R. 4 Hours when out	Orders given to patrols & by whom	Information obtained Route taken	Remarks of Patrol Leader
2/Lt E. R. Gunton	To patrol NO MANS LAND on Coy Front attempt to obtain identification by intercepting enemy patrols or stragglers — Capt Bell	Patrol left	P.31.d.8.0 at 2 am & proceeded

towards railway embankment. About 150x from our trench sounds were heard on the embankment as of a rifle being loaded. The patrol turned left along front & inspected some partly dug positions which were unoccupied. Immediately after leaving these patrol was heavily fired on by 2 M.Gs from position approx V.2.b.0.5 & V.2.b.2.8.

Patrol then proceeded along rest of Coy front returning at 3.36 am

No sign of enemy patrols were observed.

(Sgd) E.R. Gunton 2/Lt.

12-4-18

D Coy.

Patrol Report

13-4-18

Patrol leader F.E. Wilcockson Strength O.K. 4 Time when out 10pm–12.15am	Orders given to patrol & by whom	Information obtained	Patrol Leader Remarks
	To proceed E from P.31.b.6.3 towards enemy line to locate enemy posts, to engage any patrols of enemy met & if possible obtain identification Capt R.K. Spencer OC D Coy	Sgt & 9 ORs left 13 Platoon trench at 10pm & proceeded due E. We came across no sign of the enemy until we had proceeded about 600x when two Very lights were sent up from what appeared to be a system of small trenches about 100x in front of us and a MG fired a short burst, the bullets hitting the ground in front of us. We listened for some time then proceeded in a S direction for about 100x. Meeting with no signs of the enemy we returned, arriving at 12.15 am.	

Sgd F.E. Wilcockson
Sgt
13 Platoon

D Coy — Patrol Report — 13-4-18

Patrol Leader Sgt Rowley Strength OR 9 Time when out 1 am - 1.50 am	Orders given to patrol by whom	Information obtained	Patrol Leader Remarks
	To proceed from P.25.d.9 toward enemy line, to locate enemy posts, to engage any party of enemy met if possible obtain identification Capt Spencer	I & 9 other ranks left 15 Platoon trench at P.25.d.9.3 at 1 am & proceeded towards earthworks at P26 c 5 1. We met with no opposition until we had advanced to within 30x or so of trench. then we had single shots fired in our direction from a flank which proved to me that the earthworks themselves were not occupied at the time. We examined the position found a small snipers position which evidently had not been occupied very recently, on moving out towards our own lines again a M.G. opened fire but the bullets were falling short of us. We withdrew a short distance and waited for an opportunity	to go forward again, but the M.G. fire was too effective for us to get nearer. We returned to our trench line at 1.50 am. (Sgd) A. Rowley Sgt. 15 Platoon

Secret [illegible] Present [illegible] 14

12th London Regt

Movement Orders No 126

1. 175th Inf Bde will be relieved in the line by the 174th Inf Bde on the night 13/14 April & take over dispositions in the Reserve line vacated by 174th Inf Bde.

2. "The Rangers" will be relieved by the 10th London Regt & on relief will take over the area vacated by the 7th London Regt in BLANGY WOOD with Bn HQ at O.25.d.[illegible].

3. A Coy will be in reserve to receive orders of 2/10 London Regt for counter attack.

4. 2/Lt R.J. Williams with an advance party of scouts & guides will reconnoitre the dispositions in the Reserve line this afternoon.

1 Sergt per Coy will report to Bn HQ directly darkness permits of movement from forward positions. This party will proceed to a point O.25.d.7.4 [illegible] 2/Lt R.J. Williams will arrange to meet guide to Coy areas. These NCOs will be responsible for guiding their Coys to the Reserve line after relief & will meet their Coys at O.25.d.7.4

5. Guides at the rate of 1 per Platoon, 1 per Coy HQ and 2 per Bn HQ with written instructions will be ready at Bn HQ at 2.30 pm tonight 13/14. 2/Lt W.E. Ward with this party will meet incoming unit at the bridge O.25.a 65.10. at 9 pm.

6. All movement will be by platoons at 50 yards interval.

7. Details, trench stores, work in hand, will be handed over so that continuity of policy is ensured.
All orders regarding defence of the Reserve Line will be taken over from the 9th London Regt.

8. Completion of relief will be wired to Bn HQ by using the Coy Commander's name as a code word.
When the positions have been taken over in Reserve Line notification will be sent to Bn HQ the code word "BLOB" being used.

9. All heavy [illegible] will be carried out of the line by Coys.

10. The Transport Officer will arrange for [illegible] limbers to report to Battalion HQ.

[illegible] to [illegible] for the removal of signalling equipment, Carrying [illegible] etc.
[illegible] allowed [illegible].

Capt. [illegible]
[illegible] Rangers

13-4-1918

Issued to Signals at 4.15 pm.

Copy No. 1 Retained
2 175th Inf Bde
3 6th London
4 7th " "
5 2/10 " "
6 O.C. A Coy
7 B
8 C
9 D
10 HQ
11 T.O. & Q.M.
12 I.O. & M.O.
13 R.S.M.
14 } War
15 } Diary

Copy 11

"The Rangers"
12th London Regt.

Operation Orders No. 127

Ref. 62 D 1/40,000

1. The 175th Inf. Bde will be relieved in the Reserve Line by 9th Australian Bde. ~~tomorrow~~ today 15th inst.

2. The Rangers will be relieved by the 36th Bn. Australian Inf.

2. No guides are required by the incoming unit. The relief will commence at dusk

3. After relief the Bn will move to GLISY by platoons at 200 yds interval.

4. 2/Lt S.G. BEER M.C will arrange for the billeting party to meet the Bn at the ~~fork~~ Cross roads N.26.c.6.3.

5. Transport will be required as follows.

(a) 1 Limber and Cookers horses for A Coy. O/C A Coy will post guide on road at O.25 d.8.3.

(b) Medical Cart at RAP at approx. O.25.C.5.4.
Water carts to be removed from approx same place

(c) 2 Limbers to convey baggage ~~& to~~ ~~which will be dumped~~ at approx. N.30.d.0.0. RSM will post guide on main road ~~and will also~~ to meet ~~[illegible]~~ ~~[illegible]~~ limber. He will also arrange that all baggage from A, B C & D Coys is dumped at this place by 7.45 pm.

(d) Lewis Gun limbers for B C & D Coys will meet Coys at —

(e) Cookers will be removed from same site as emplaced yesterday.

6. QM will arrange that all blankets & valises etc are dumped at billets in CLISY.

7. All tents and bivouacs will be left standing in present positions, handed over on relief

and receipts obtained, which will be handed in to Bn HQ at GLISY on arrival.

8. Completion of relief will be reported to Bn HQ. in the line by runner.

Issued to Signals at 2pm 15 + 18

Copy No 1 Retained
2 OC 3rd Australian
3 OC A
4 B
5 C
6 D
7 HQ.
8 T.O. + Q.M.
9 Mot Ben MO
10 R.S.M.

9

Instructions regarding War Diaries and Intelligence Summaries are contained in F. S. Regs., Part II. and the Staff Manual respectively. Title pages will be prepared in manuscript.

WAR DIARY
or
INTELLIGENCE SUMMARY.
(Erase heading not required.)

Vol 17

Army Form C. 2118.

Place	Date	Hour	Summary of Events and Information	Remarks and references to Appendices
			War Diary The Rangers 12th London Reg Volume V May 1918	

D. D. & L., London, E.C.
(A10266) Wt W5300/P713 750,000 2/15 Sch. 52 Forms/C2118/16

Army Form C. 2118.

Instructions regarding War Diaries and Intelligence Summaries are contained in F. S. Regs., Part II. and the Staff Manual respectively. Title pages will be prepared in manuscript.

WAR DIARY
or
INTELLIGENCE SUMMARY.
(Erase heading not required.)

Place	Date	Hour	Summary of Events and Information	Remarks and references to Appendices
CACHY	24-4-18	5 am	After heavy bombardment along whole of front, the enemy attacked with infantry and tanks were reported to have reached Eastern outskirts of CACHY.	
		4 PM	Battalion counter-attacked in conjunction with troops on flanks ~~reached objectives successfully~~	
			Bn HQ moved forward and established themselves in Quarry at east edge of CACHY.	
	25-4-18	8.30 AM		
		11.30 PM	Bn relieved by French Moroccan Troops. moved back - Bn HQ opened in Quarry in DOMART VALLEY.	
	26-4-18		Heavy shelling by enemy inflicting many casualties. - Capt L K SPENCER handed over command of "D" Coy. to Lieut A A BAKER, + took over duties of Adjutant -	
		12 mid.	2 French Bns of 165 French Division relieved Battalion + relief completed by 1.30 am 27th	
	27-4-18	3.30 am	Bn reached destination, i.e Copse one mile E of BOIS DE BLANGY.	
		11 am	Bn moved off to embus at AMIENS arriving at BUSSUS late in afternoon -	
BUSSUS near ABBEVILLE			Casualties during above period were :- Killed 2 Officers 40 or; Wounded 5 " 132 or; Gassed 1 " 10 or; Missing - - 8 or.	
	28-4-18		Bn cleaning up. - Church parade on Village Green	
	29-4-18		Cleaning up + refitting	
	30-4-18		Training during morning	
	1-5-18 } 2-5-18 }		Training during morning - 44 or transferred by order of DIVISION to 6th LONDON REGT + party proceeded to join on 2/5/18	
	3-5-18		Training and Range Practice - Inspection of Transport by G.O.C 175th Inf Bde.	
	4-5-18		MAJOR J.H.L DAY (11th LR temp. att. to Bn) and 32 ors. proceeded to VILLERS-SOUS-AILLY, III CORPS R.T.C as Battn Surplus -	
	5-5-18		Transport moved by road to BAISIEUX, staging at BOURDON area and continuing on 6th to BAISIEUX	
	6-5-18	7.45 AM	Battalion moved off from Billets at BUSSUS, marched to AILLY LE HAUT CLOCHER and embussed for BAISIEUX	
		7 pm	Battalion arrived + bivouacced at BOIS ROBERT immediately SW of BAISIEUX village -	
	8-5-18	2 pm	Battalion moved to CORPS RESERVE LINE, 1000 yds east of WARLOY - Bn HQ at V. 19c 3.7 (Sheet 57d)	
	9-5-18		Lieut Colonel S. CHART DSO took over command of Bn from Major E.P. CAWSTON (87 RIR)	

(A7092). Wt. W12839/M1293. 750,000. 1/17. D. D. & L., Ltd. Forms/C.2118/14.

Instructions regarding War Diaries and Intelligence Summaries are contained in F. S. Regs., Part II. and the Staff Manual respectively. Title pages will be prepared in manuscript.

WAR DIARY
or
INTELLIGENCE SUMMARY.
(Erase heading not required.)

Army Form C. 2118.

Place	Date	Hour	Summary of Events and Information	Remarks and references to Appendices
WARLOY	10-5-18		Major E.P CAWSTON returned to 2/10th LONDON REGT. All men of Battalion bathed at VADENCOURT BATHS	
	11-5-18		Bn engaged on improving trenches &c Working party of 150 men employed by Bde under REs to improve defences of sector.	
	12-5-18		Capt LK Spencer handed over duties of Adjutant to LIEUT D.H LYAL, and assumed command of "D" Coy. Lieut HE CLARKE assumed command of "C" Coy – Working party of 150 men employed by Brigade under REs to improve defences –	
	13-5-18		Working party of 150 men employed by Brigade under REs for improvement of defences of sector.	
	14th and 15th		– ditto – – ditto – – ditto –	
	16/5/18		Relieved by 24th LONDON REGT in Corps Reserve – Relief completed 9pm – Moved forward into Brigade Reserve relieving 20th LONDON REGT – Night quiet. Disposition:– "B" Coy Forward – Melbourne Trench – A & C Coys – Murray Trench – D Coy in Maze – Bn HQ in Maze at V.24 d 1.3 Sheet 57d SE	
	17-5-18		48 men sent to Advanced BDE HQ for work with Tunnellers & to live there – 4 shifts of 12 men to work under REs on new BN H.Q for Support Bn. 3 Coys working 10PM – 2AM on MELBOURNE TRENCH & CAREY TRENCH.	
	18th & 19th		– ditto – – ditto – – ditto –	
	20-5-18		Relieved 9th LONDON REGT as RIGHT FRONT BN. – Relief completed 12.30 am "B" Coy on left – "A" Coy on right "C" Coy in Support – "D" Coy in Reserve with BN HQ in MELBOURNE TRENCH.	
	21-5-18		Working on trench system –	
WARLOY	22-5-18		Relieved by 2/2nd LONDON REGT & returned to DIVISIONAL RESERVE at WARLOY in billets – Relief completed 12.30 am – Reported in at 3.30 am –	
	23rd to 27th		In Billets at WARLOY as Counter attack Battalion – 24th – Bn working from 10PM – 2AM on MELBOURNE & SYDNEY STREETS.	
	27-5-18		Bn relieved 8th LONDON REGT in the line, leaving WARLOY about 8PM Relief complete 1am – Dispositions "C" & "D" Coys in front line, "A" Coy in Support, "B" In Reserve. Night quiet –	
	28, 29 & 30th		In line – Tour was quiet – Three forward Coys worked 4 hrs nightly on improving & wiring trenches – Reserve Coy worked on tunnelled dug out & provided carrying parties for 2 front Coys –	
	31-5-18		Relieved by 7th BUFFS REGT & returned to Bivouac Camp at C.20.b.5.5. – Relief completed 12.30 am	

Stephen Chart
Lieut Colonel
Comdg "The Rangers" 12th London Regt

(A7092). Wt. W12539/M1293. 750,000. 1/17. D. D. & L., Ltd. Forms/C.2118/14.

VR 18

Confidential

The Rangers 12th London Regt

War Diary

From 1st June to 30th June
1918

Army Form C. 2118.

Instructions regarding War Diaries and Intelligence Summaries are contained in F. S. Regs., Part II. and the Staff Manual respectively. Title pages will be prepared in manuscript.

WAR DIARY
or
INTELLIGENCE SUMMARY.

(Erase heading not required.)

Place	Date	Hour	Summary of Events and Information	Remarks and references to Appendices
C 20 b 5.5 Sheet 62d.	1st June		Battalion resting and cleaning up	
	2nd "		Cleaning up Camp + training under Coy arrangements	
	3 + 4th		Training under Coy arrangements	
B 15. b 5.3. Sheet 62d.	5th June	5 pm	Battalion moved to Wood at B 15. b 5.3	
	6th "		Training under Coy arrangements + improvements to new camp	
	7th "		Range practice	
	8th "		Training under Coy arrangements	
	9th "		Church parade	
	10th	7 am	Battalion moved from present area + marched to VILLERS-BOCAGE, embussing at 10 am	
PISSY			Arrived in billets at PISSY at 3 30 pm. Billets generally were very good. Entered 22nd Corps - G.H.Q. Reserve.	
	11th + 12th		Training under Coy arrangements - "A" Coy on range at P 29. b. 0.6 - Reconnaissance of various sectors of French Army front carried out daily by some officers.	
	13th		- ditto - - Platoon demonstration on Range. Bn. Sports in the evening.	
	14th		- ditto -	
	15th	8.30 am	Battalion route march	
		11.30	Training under Coy arrangements	
	16th		Church Parade.	
	17th		Training under Coy arrangements - "B" Coy on Range	
	18th	2 pm	Battalion moved from PISSY by march route + embussed at BRIQUEMESNIL, debussing at B. 9.a central Sheet 62d at 6 pm + marched to Camp in Wood approximately at B. 8. b. 8.3. relieving 2/4th LONDON REGT. Re-entered IIIrd Corps.	
C. 21. b. Sheet 62d NW	19th	7 pm	Battalion left Camp by march route to Camp at C. 21. b relieving 2/4th LONDON REGT in Divisional reserve	
	20th		Battalion improving Camp - + training under Coy arrangements.	
	21st		Training under Coy arrangements - 1 Platoon "B" Coy reported to Area Commandant BEAUCOURT to erect YMCA Marquee in DAILY MAIL WOOD	

(A7092). Wt. W12839/M1293. 750,000. 1/17. D. D. & L., Ltd. Forms/C.2118/14.

Instructions regarding War Diaries and Intelligence Summaries are contained in F. S. Regs., Part II. and the Staff Manual respectively. Title pages will be prepared in manuscript.

WAR DIARY
or
INTELLIGENCE SUMMARY.
(Erase heading not required.)

Army Form C. 2118.

Place	Date	Hour	Summary of Events and Information	Remarks and references to Appendices
C 21.b. Sheet 62d	22-6-18 and 24-6-18		Training under Coy arrangements.	
	25-6-18	8pm	Battalion moved forward + relieved 8th London Regt in support position – Major EC Fortescue rejoined Bn from Transport Lines to take over command vice Lt Col S CHART DSO in temporary command of 173rd Infantry Bde.	
	26-6-18 to 25-6-18		Battalion engaged upon working parties for deepening, fire stepping + wiring DOLLY TRENCH also crop cutting	
	28-6-18	11pm	Bn moved forward into front line trench system + relieved (Q.V.R.) 9th LONDON REGT. Relief complete 1.5 am. Dispositions A Coy Right. B Coy Centre. C Coy Left. D Coy Reserve.	
	29-30-6-18		In line. Period quiet. Work done nightly in deepening and firestepping trenches. Two patrols out nightly.	

E C Fortescue
Major
Comdg "The Rangers" 12th London Regt

Instructions regarding War Diaries and Intelligence Summaries are contained in F. S. Regs., Part II. and the Staff Manual respectively. Title pages will be prepared in manuscript.

WAR DIARY
or
~~INTELLIGENCE SUMMARY.~~

(Erase heading not required.)

Army Form C. 2118.

WR 19

Place	Date	Hour	Summary of Events and Information	Remarks and references to Appendices
			Volume 7	
			"The Rangers" 12th London Regt.	
			July 1st 1918 to July 31st 1918	

D. D. & L., London, E.C.
(A10266) Wt W5300/P713 750,000 2/18 Sch. 52 Forms/C2118/16

Instructions regarding War Diaries and Intelligence Summaries are contained in F. S. Regs., Part II. and the Staff Manual respectively. Title pages will be prepared in manuscript.

WAR DIARY
or
INTELLIGENCE SUMMARY.
(Erase heading not required.)

Army Form C. 2118.

Place	Date	Hour	Summary of Events and Information	Remarks and references to Appendices
In line SENLIS SECTOR	1-7-18 to 5-7-18		Battalion in front line trenches – Working parties nightly deepening & fire stepping trenches – Two patrols out nightly	
	6-7-18		Battalion relieved by 2nd LONDON REGT in the line + returned to Divisional Reserve relieving 3rd LONDON REGT. – Battalion HQ at D.9.b.5.6 Sheet 62D. – {Disposition B+D Coys forward in LAVIEVILLE LINE, A+C Coy in STRAW TRENCH.	
	7-7-18		Working party of "A" Coy assisting Tunnelling Coy –	
	8-7-18	9.10 PM	Received orders for "Battle Station Practice" to take place. – Companies moved off to Battle Positions	
	9-7-18	12.50 AM	Received orders from 175th Inf Bde to resume Normal Positions –	
			Battalion engaged upon working party, wiring revetting + deepening LAVIEVILLE LINE.	
	10-7-18 } 11-7-18 }		ditto -ditto- -ditto- from 9.30 pm to 3 am.	
			Lieut Col. S. CHART D.S.O assumed command of Battalion on return from 173rd Inf Bde.	
	12/13 July		Relieved 6TH LONDON REGT in Brigade Reserve. – Battalion disposed in trenches. Period quiet. Battalion working nightly on forward trenches digging and wiring.	
	16/17 July		Relieved 2/10th LONDON REGT in the Left sub-sector of Brigade Front. Relief complete 2.40 am Disposition "B" + "D" Coys Front Line, "A" Coy Support, "C" Coy Reserve. – Position Right of ALBERT – AMIENS ROAD. – Period generally quiet – Right Front Coy TM + shelled intermittently. Battalion HQ shelled + received attention of enemy machine guns.	
	21/22		"A" Coy relieved "B" Coy – 5 Australians attached to give instruction in patrolling – Accompanied patrols nightly to German Front Line. One Coy of each Regiment – 1st, 2nd + 3rd Bns 132nd American Infantry, attached for instruction for 48 hours Bn HQ 1st Bn also attached for 48 hours	
	24/25		Large number of Gas Shells in the area – 23 cases sent down from Gas	

(A7092). Wt. W12839/M1295. 750,000. 1/17. D. D. & L., Ltd. Forms/C.2118/14.

Instructions regarding War Diaries and Intelligence Summaries are contained in F. S. Regs., Part II. and the Staff Manual respectively. Title pages will be prepared in manuscript.

WAR DIARY
or
INTELLIGENCE SUMMARY.
(Erase heading not required.)

Army Form C. 2118.

Place	Date	Hour	Summary of Events and Information	Remarks and references to Appendices
SENLIS SECTOR	July 26/17		Relieved by 23RD LONDON REGT - Relief complete 12.30 am. Returned to BOIS ROBERT - under canvas -	
	27th		Cleaning up + 1 Coy bathed at AGNICOURT BATHS	
	28th		Moved from BOIS ROBERT to ROUND WOOD under canvas. Remainder of Battalion bathed.	
	29th		Attended demonstration of attack by tanks at VAUX. Battalion (500 strong) embussed at 7am - returned to Camp 7 pm - "A" + "C" Coys practised attack. -	
	30th		Relieved 8TH LONDON REGT in Reserve position - Battalion accommodated in tents and "biovies" - Relief complete 9 pm. Position ST. LAWRENCE VALLEY D.19.a.	
	31st		Relieved 2ND BN 132 Inf Regt (American) in the line - Left sub-sector of Left Brigade - 47th DIV. (24th LONDON REGT) on left - 3RD BN (U.S.) relieved 10TH LONDON REGT same night. - Position left near ALBERT-AMIENS ROAD. - - "A", "B" + "C" Coys Front Line "D" Coy in support.	

Stephen Chart

Lieut Colonel

Comdg "The Rangers" 12th London Regt

(A7092). Wt. W12839/M1293. 750,000. 1/17. D. D. & L., Ltd. Forms/C.2118/14.

175th Bde.

58th Div.

12th BATTALION

LONDON REGIMENT (THE RANGERS)

A U G U S T 1 9 1 8

11

Confidential

WD 20

War Diary

Volume VIII

Aug 1st – 31st 1918

The Rangers, 12 London Regt.

Instructions regarding War Diaries and Intelligence Summaries are contained in F. S. Regs., Part II. and the Staff Manual respectively. Title pages will be prepared in manuscript.

WAR DIARY
or
INTELLIGENCE SUMMARY.
(Erase heading not required.)

Army Form C. 2118.

Place	Date	Hour	Summary of Events and Information	Remarks and references to Appendices
TRENCHES SENLIS SECTOR	July 31st Aug 1st/18		Relieved 2nd American Battalion 132nd Regiment in Left sub sector of Brigade Front – Immediately South of ALBERT-AMIENS Rd – Disposition "A", "B" & "C" Coy in Front Line – "D" Coy in support.	
	2-8-18		About 4.30 am a big explosion was heard in quarry in enemy lines on right Front – Other indications to suggest enemy had retired –	
		1 pm.	"A" + "C" Coys pushed forward patrols to old enemy front line + found them unoccupied –	
		5 pm	"A" + "C" Coys pushed forward patrols to old enemy support line + further without interference – Observation post established in old Boche Front line	
	3-8-18		"D" Coy pushed forward patrols at 10 am + 4 pm to River ANCRE + reported all clear. Posts established in old Boche Front Lines – Relieved by 7th QUEENS REGT. Relief complete 2.45 am –	
	3/4th		Marched straight from Line to buses near BAIZIEUX – Embussed at 6 am. + conveyed to VIGNACOURT to billets	
VIGNACOURT	5th 6th + 7th		Refitting and bathing.	
BOIS ESCARDONNEUSE	7th/8th	9 pm	Embussed + conveyed to FRANVILLERS – Debussed + marched to BOIS ESCARDONNEUSE arriving 1.30 am	
	8th		Under one hour's notice – Battle Stores issued	
		1 pm	Moved off behind 9th LONDON REGT – through BONNAY to BALLARAT TRENCH J.10 & 17 (62D) Remained there until 11 pm. – C.O. reported to 36th Inf Bde HQ at 9 pm + ordered to close up gap in line or assemble in K.26. – Companies proceeded independantly – and	
	9th		Rendezvous at 4.30 am at K.25d. – No gap in line –	
FRONT LINE Nr MORLANCOURT		4.50 pm	Orders received to attack – "B" + "D" Coys in front line – "C" + "A" Coys in support –	
		5.30 pm	ZERO. – Objective line K.11.c.3.1. – K.17 central – The 131st AMERICAN REGT co-operating on Right – 8th London Regt on left 5TH BERKS REGT in support.	

(A7092). Wt. W12839/M1293. 750,000. 1/17. D. D. & L., Ltd. Forms/C.2118/14.

Instructions regarding War Diaries and Intelligence Summaries are contained in F. S. Regs., Part II. and the Staff Manual respectively. Title pages will be prepared in manuscript.

WAR DIARY
or
INTELLIGENCE SUMMARY.
(Erase heading not required.)

Army Form C. 2118.

Place	Date	Hour	Summary of Events and Information	Remarks and references to Appendices
FRONT LINE NR MORLANCOURT	9-8-18	8pm	Battalion reached line of road K.16.d.95. – Americans up on right – Troops on left, position uncertain	
		9pm	All Companies reached objective + consolidating. About 250 Prisoners.	
			O.C. Coys: A: Lieut R.C.R. BENNETT. B. 2/Lt (A/Capt) E.R. GURTON. C. Lieut (A/Capt) H.E. CLARKE. D. Lieut. G.C. BEECHING.	
	9/10th		Patrols pushed forward at night all along front to locate enemy –	
			9th LONDON REGT moved into support – 5th BERKS REGT in support of 8th LONDON REGT.	
			One Company of 9th LONDON REGT reinforced the "RANGERS"	
	10th	6.45am	Reconnoitring patrol pushed well forward to ascertain line held by enemy –	
		11am	2/Lt L DUCKETT i/c patrol sent back message stating he was in touch with enemy at K 12. b 2.2	
		4.30pm	Battalion took over portion of new line established by 9th LONDON REGT + elements of AMERICANS. Companies disposed "A" Coy in front line, "B" in close support, "D" earmarked for counter-attack, "C" in Reserve	
	11th 12th		Dispositions of Battalion remained the same until relieved by 23rd LONDON REGT 47th DIVISION.	
	13th		Battalion moved back after relief to J.17.b central (approx) + remained here until relieved by 21st LONDON REGT. –	
		4.30pm	Battalion moved off + marched to BOIS ESCARDONNEUSE (CORPS RESERVE)	
BOIS ESCARDONNEUSE	14-17		Cleaning up, bathing, training + range practice.	
	18th		Church Parade – Inspection by new B.G.C. 175th Inf. Bde –	
	19th		Battalion training + range practice – Inspection of Transport + Battalion by B.G.C 175th Inf. Bde	
			Draft of 6 Officers + 227 o.r. joined Unit from KRRC – Majority of the men with 2 and 3 yrs service –	
	20th		Battalion training –	
			Major J.M. Samson (2/2 London Regt att) took over command of Battalion vice Lieut Col S. Chart D.S.O. to UK on leave.	
	21st		Orders were received from Brigade that Battalion were to be in readiness to proceed forward at short notice – Extra ammunition issued to Companies. CAPT. F.B. CUBITT joined as Second-in-Command	
J.12 (Sheet 62D)	22nd		Reveille 4.[redacted] am – Battalion moved off 5.20am for J.12. arriving at 8 [redacted] am.	
			Remained at J.12 all day awaiting orders.	
			Battalion ordered to "Stand to" – Enemy counter-attacking 47th Division –	
TAILLES WOOD			Battalion moved to TAILLES WOOD at midnight.	

(A7092). Wt. W12839/M1293. 750,000. 1/17. D. D. & L., Ltd. Forms/C.2118/14.

Army Form C. 2118.

WAR DIARY
or
INTELLIGENCE SUMMARY.
(*Erase heading not required.*)

Instructions regarding War Diaries and Intelligence Summaries are contained in F. S. Regs., Part II. and the Staff Manual respectively. Title pages will be prepared in manuscript.

Place	Date	Hour	Summary of Events and Information	Remarks and references to Appendices
TAILLES WOOD	23-8-18		Moved from position round TAILLES WOOD to assembly positions) – ~~Road line through~~ L.2.a. O.C. Coys A. Lieut. R.C.R. BENNETT. B. Lieut R.B. LOVELESS. C. LIEUT. S.C. NUNN. D. LIEUT. L.S. DICKENS.	
	24-8-18	1 am	Battalion went into attack with 47th DIVISION – Objective, Railway Line CHALK PIT L.1.d.5.5 along F.28.a.2.7. – Brigade reached line of road through 27 b + d. to CHALK PIT – Headquarters in Quarry L.1.b.3.1 moved to HAPPY VALLEY. 100 Prisoners.	
HAPPY VALLEY	25th	2.30 am	Battalion went into attack – Objective TRIGGER WOOD – No resistance – Line consolidated. Relieved by 7th LONDON REGT withdrawn to Ravine in F. 28 c. – arrived 2.15 am on 26th	
F. 28 c	26th + 27th		Refitting and resting	
	27th ~~28th~~	12 noon	Moved to BRONFAY FARM – positions of readiness – in support to 173rd + 174th Infantry Brigades –	
	28th ~~29th~~		Relieved 6th LONDON REGT in line A. 23 + 24 at 1.30 am (Sheet 62c) Pushed out outpost line to RED FARM – no opposition – Patrol pushed out to BATTERY COPSE under Lieut. BEECHING.	
		5 pm	Moved forward as a Brigade to B.20. – Reached there 7.40 pm Headquarters: BATTERY COPSE. 1/4th SUFFOLKS + 2/10th LONDONS in Trench Line through B.21. 9th + 12th LONDONS in Trench Line in B.20. in line B.20. – Headquarters at SPINNEY "B" – Moved forward at	
B. 20.	30th	12 noon	4th Suffolk Regt + 10th LONDON REGT 1st wave – 9th + 12th LONDON REGT 2nd wave. Objective 2nd Wave Ridge beyond MARRIERES WOOD. Whole line held up by M. Guns on Ridge B.18 + 24. Australians on right also held up.	
	31st		Battalion at B.18 + 24 – 174th Infantry Bde passed through at dawn and took MARRIERES WOOD to grid line C.19 – 20. Battalion moved back to valley ~~—~~ near MARICOURT ~~—~~ after being relieved by Unit of 74th DIVISION Arrived at 10 pm.	
			Total Casualties for Action of 9/8/18. Officers "Killed" – 2/Lt W. Lambourne (23rd London Regt att) "Died of Wds" – 2/Lt KT Harben (5th —"—), 2/Lt S. Tucker MM (20th —"—)	
			Officers "Wounded" 2/Lt (A/Capt) ER Gurton, 2/Lt AH Wright (13th —"—), Lieut (A/Capt) HE Clarke, Lieut RW Tanant	
			Other Ranks "Killed" 10 "Died of Wounds" 2 "Wounded" 133 Wdd (at Duty) 5 Missing 8	

(A7092). Wt. W12839/M1293. 750,000. 1/17. D. D. & L., Ltd. Forms/C.2118/14.

Instructions regarding War Diaries and Intelligence Summaries are contained in F. S. Regs., Part II. and the Staff Manual respectively. Title pages will be prepared in manuscript.

WAR DIARY
or
INTELLIGENCE SUMMARY.
(Erase heading not required.)

Army Form C. 2118.

Place	Date	Hour	Summary of Events and Information	Remarks and references to Appendices
August	1918.		Total Casualties of Actions of 24th to 31st inclusive	

Officers

Killed	Lieut	R.C.R.B	Bennett	(20th L.R att)
	2/Lt	E.G	Johnson	(1st LR ")
Died of Wounds	2/Lt	E.R	Barton	(1st LR ")
	2/Lt	J.D.	Sullivan	(24th LR ")
Wounded	2/Lt	O.	Glendinning	(1st LR att)
	2/Lt	WTS	Garnham	—"—
	2/Lt	WHS	Grosvenor	—"—
	2/Lt	CC	Veitch	(7th LR att)
	2/Lt	DKB	Williams	(24th LR att)
	Lieut	I.S	Dickins	(13th LR att)

Other Ranks

Killed	31
Died of Wounds	8
Wounded	202
Missing "believed prisoner"	2
Missing	18
Wounded (at Duty)	8

Reinforcements (new – all ranks) August.

Date	Offs.	OR	
14th	2	1	2/Lt E.G JOHNSON (1 LR att) 2/Lt CC VEITCH (7th LR)
19th	6	229	2/Lt O. GLENDINNING, 2/Lt WTS GARNHAM, 2/Lt WHS GROSVENOR, 2/Lt WE BARTON and 2/Lt RE MALLISON (all 1st LR att) Lt RS LOVELESS
22nd	-	2	Major J.P. CRITCHLEY (1/4th KOYLI att)
25th	1	-	
27th	-	2	
29th	2	2	2/Lt WG DAVISON (1st LR att) 2/Lt E.H PALMER
TOTAL	11	236	

Ned P Corbitt [signature]
Capt
Comdg "The Rangers" 12th London Regt.

(A7092). Wt. W12839/M1293 750,000. 1/17. D. D. & L., Ltd. Forms/C.2118/14.

Instructions regarding War Diaries and Intelligence Summaries are contained in F. S. Regs., Part II. and the Staff Manual respectively. Title pages will be prepared in manuscript.

WAR DIARY
or
INTELLIGENCE SUMMARY.
(Erase heading not required.)

12 London Regt 175/58
Vol 21

Army Form C. 2118.

Place	Date	Hour	Summary of Events and Information	Remarks and references to Appendices
MARICOURT	Sept 1st 1918		Battalion cleaning up and resting in valley near MARICOURT-SUR-SOMME – Companies bathed in the River Somme –	
	2nd – 5th		Battalion training + at Range practice	
			Major S J M SAMPSON M.C (2/2nd LONDON REGT) returned to his Unit and CAPT F.B CUBITT assumed command during absence (on leave) of Lieut Colonel S. CHART DSO.	
	6th		Orders received that the Brigade were relieving Brigade of 47th Division in the line tonight	
			Battalion moved off + embussed at 4 pm – Relieved Battalion of 47th DIV in the line near AIZECOURT L'ABBE at LIERMONT TRENCH D.12.c (Sheet 57D)	
	7th		Brigade pushed forward 7000 yards.	
	8th		Battalion withdrew at darkness to positions just in front of LIERMONT, near GUYENCOURT – Line taken over by 74th DIV.	
	9th		Resting.	
EPEHY	10th		Attack on EPEHY by 173rd Inf Bde unsuccessful – Battalion took over part of the line at night.	
	11th		In front of EPEHY – 9th + 10th Bns joined Battalion in the Line –	
	11/12th		Enemy put down box barrage + attacked TATTENHAM POST. "D" Coy were surrounded + post taken.	
	13th		Relieved by Suffolks + went into Support.	
BOIS EPINETTE	15th		Relieved by 6th LONDON REGT – Moved to BOIS EPINETTE.	
	16+17th		Battalion Resting	
GUYENCOURT	18th		Moved to GUYENCOURT into Corps Reserve.	
	20th		Moved forward –	
	21st		Attack by 9th + 12th Battalions + took KILDARE AVENUE. – Troops on left held up –	
	22nd		Holding on to KILDARE AV. – 9th LONDON REGT passed through 21.30 with 1 Coy 4th SUFFOLK REGT and took KILDARE POST – No opposition –	

(A7092). Wt. W12839/M1293. 750,000. 1/17. D. D. & L., Ltd. Forms/C.2118/14

Instructions regarding War Diaries and Intelligence Summaries are contained in F. S. Regs., Part II. and the Staff Manual respectively. Title pages will be prepared in manuscript.

WAR DIARY
or
INTELLIGENCE SUMMARY.
(Erase heading not required.)

Army Form C. 2118.

Place	Date	Hour	Summary of Events and Information	Remarks and references to Appendices
	24-9-18		Relieved by 5th BERKS REGT 12th DIV. & marched back to VILLERS – Embussed at 0530 to TRONES WOOD – Billeted outside the Wood in small shelters.	
TRONES WOOD	26th		Bn resting – Left by march route 2030 to DERNACOURT	
	27th		Travelled by rail from DERNACOURT 0130 to AUBIGNY arriving at 2230 [illegible] hours.	
	28th		Bn marched to ESTREE CAUCHIE arriving in billets at 1330.	
ESTREE CAUCHIE	29th		Bn resting.	
	30th		Moved by march route to CAMBLAIN L'ABBE – Embussed at 1030 and debussed at SOUCHEZ Proceeded by march route to Support position in LIEVIN and ANGRES.	

A. [illegible]
Lieut Colonel
Comdg "The Rangers" 12th London Regt

(A7092). Wt. W12839 M1293. 750,000. 1/17. D. D. & L., Ltd. Forms/C.2118/14.

9 — 12 London Rg — Oct 18 — 22 — 58

Instructions regarding War Diaries and Intelligence Summaries are contained in F. S. Regs., Part II. and the Staff Manual respectively. Title pages will be prepared in manuscript.

Army Form C. 2118.

WAR DIARY
or
INTELLIGENCE SUMMARY.
(Erase heading not required.)

Place	Date	Hour	Summary of Events and Information	Remarks and references to Appendices
LIEVIN & ANGRES	1/10/18		Battalion training – Lewis Gunners, Signallers + in Musketry.	
	2nd		"A" Company moved into Support of a Battalion of KRR's (20th DIV)	
	3rd + 4th		Battalion – training –	
	5th		"A" Company rejoined during morning – 3 Companies working in LENS, clearing up streets.	
	6th		Church Parade – Musketry – Platoon competitions, Won by HQ team –	
	7th		Rifle competition Coy HQ's – won by "B" Coy – Companies bathing –	
	8/9th		Relieved 6th Bn in the line – right sector Left Brigade – near ANNAY – "B" + "D" Coys forward – "A" + "C" Companies in support – Relief completed 2215.	
Nr ANNAY	9/10th		"A" Company moved forward to undertake patrolling of Front – "D" Coy 9th Bn moved into Support under command of O C "Rangers" –	
	10th		Quiet day – Enemy shelling Coke ovens – Night patrols located enemy – Enemy shelling at night above normal –	
	11th		Afternoon patrol found enemy lines vacated – Lieut Col. S CHART DSO wounded by bullet in leg. CAPT GMG WYATT assumed command (temporarily)	
	12th		Lt Col. AD. DERVISH-JONES DSO. MC. took over command – After patrolling "A" Coy moved forward at 0100 + took up positions in ANNAY – MONTIGNY SWITCH (1000 yds advance) "B" + "D" Coys established supporting posts – no opposition encountered – At 1430 in conjunction with 10th Bn on left "A" Coy moved forward to line of road ANNAY in 1.31.b 5.5. Sheet 44a (1000 yds advance) "B" Coy moved up into positions vacated by "A" Coy – "B" Coy sent out patrols to Canal + located enemy MG's in 1.26. Relieved by 3 Coys of 7/8 KOSB – Relief complete 0400 hrs 13th – Bn moved back to CITE AUGUSTÉ	
	13th		Marched to FOUQUIERES and billeted in village	

(A7092). Wt. W12839/M1293. 750,000. 1/17. D. D. & L., Ltd. Forms/C.2118/14.

Army Form C. 2118.

Instructions regarding War Diaries and Intelligence Summaries are contained in F. S. Regs., Part II. and the Staff Manual respectively. Title pages will be prepared in manuscript.

WAR DIARY
or
INTELLIGENCE SUMMARY.
(Erase heading not required.)

Place	Date	Hour	Summary of Events and Information	Remarks and references to Appendices
FOUQUIERES	13/10/18		Accommodated in ruined houses & cellars. – Moved off at 1200 – arrived 1600.	
	14th & 15th		Lieut Col AD DERVISH-JONES DSO.MC. left to take over command of 8th LONDON REGT. Battalion rested & cleaned up – Lt Col. A. GROVER D.S.O. M.C. 1st Bedfordshire Regiment, arrived to take over command	
	16th		Moved into COURRIERES into Billets	
	17th		Enemy retired – 9th Bn followed to MONCHEAUX but failed to establish touch – The Rangers left COURRIERES 14.30 hours & marched via OSTRICOURT and LE FOREST relieving 9th LONDON REGT in MONCHEAUX –	
	18th		Advance continued – 12th LONDON REGT – Advance guard reached line PT de BREUVY 0830 hours (Sheet 44a) B. C & A Coys pushed out as outpost line – Enemy MGs encountered in front of wood from BRODERIE line. "C" Coy pushed posts forward into BRODERIE in front "A" Coy established post in LA CARDONNERIE – Considerable shelling of our front posts Enemy retired at dawn –	
	20th		Advance continued – Advance guard 9th Bn., "The RANGERS" at head of main body – Advance guard reached RUMEGIES – 12th Bn billetted for night at HAUT HAMEAU (Sheet 44) No resistance encountered –	
	19th		Advance continued – 2/10th Bn Advance guard – 12th Bn in Main body – Advance guard reach NOMAIN. – "The Rangers" billetted in LA PLANQUE at 1800 hours.	
	21st		The Battalion as Advance Guard passed through 9th at RUMEGIES at 0730 hours – After advancing 4000 yards "B" Coy on the right came under heavy MG fire from isolated houses and were held up – "D" Coy on left passed through first objective & advanced another 500 yards when held up by enemy MG fire in front of FORT DE MAULDE – During afternoon "B" Coy. were enabled to establish a forward post in CENSE de CHOQUES. – "A" & "C" Coys. moved into support of "B" & "D" Coys respectively – No further advance possible –	

(A7092). Wt. W12839/M1293. 750,000. 1/17. D. D. & L., Ltd. Forms/C.2118/14.

Instructions regarding War Diaries and Intelligence Summaries are contained in F. S. Regs., Part II. and the Staff Manual respectively. Title pages will be prepared in manuscript.

WAR DIARY
or
INTELLIGENCE SUMMARY.
(Erase heading not required.)

Army Form C. 2118.

Place	Date	Hour	Summary of Events and Information	Remarks and references to Appendices
CENSE de CHOQUES (Sheet 44.)	22 10/18		At 0500 hours A + B Coys endeavoured to move forward to canal bank in conjunction with DIVISION on right - They encountered heavy MG fire + wire in front of FORT + were compelled to withdraw - The 2/10th LONDON REGT took over the right sector of Brigade front - "A" + B Coys were withdrawn into Support at QUESNOY - "C" Coy relieved "D" in outpost line + pushed out patrols who got into touch with the enemy in front of the FORT - "D" Coy withdrew into QUESNOY.	
RUMEGIES.	23rd		Relieved by 9th LONDON REGT - Relief complete 2030 hours - Marched back to RUMEGIES and occupied billets at 0630 hours on 24th	
-"-	24-25		Resting + training - Village, near Church, shelled necessitating evacuation of that portion on night of 25th	
	26th		Resting + training -	
AIX	27th		Bn moved by march route at 0230 hrs to AIX into billets, arrived about 0400 hours	
	28th		Battalion training - Musketry, Coy attack schemes + forming out post lines - Specialist training -	
	29th		-ditto- Coys on Range - Musketry, Coy drill, Guard duties, Bayonet fighting - 1 Sgt + 2 Section Commanders per Coy proceeded to RUMEGIES for training under RE's in raft making.	
	30th		-ditto- -ditto-	
	31st		-ditto- -ditto- - Training also included Artillery Formation drill -	
			Casualties during month as follows:-	
			Officers "Killed" NIL	
			Officers "Wounded" Lt Col S. CHART DSO; 2/Lt. J.P. GRENE (2nd Leinster Regt att)	
			Officers "Missing" NIL	
			Other ranks "KILLED" 2	
			-"- "DIED of WOUNDS" 4	
			-"- "WOUNDED" 29	
			-"- "WDD and DUTY" 1	
			-"- "MISSING" NIL	

Army Form C. 2118.

Instructions regarding War Diaries and Intelligence Summaries are contained in F. S. Regs., Part II. and the Staff Manual respectively. Title pages will be prepared in manuscript.

WAR DIARY
or
INTELLIGENCE SUMMARY.
(Erase heading not required.)

Place	Date	Hour	Summary of Events and Information	Remarks and references to Appendices
			DRAFTS arrived during month:-	
			Lieut N P De Saulles } 15 10/18	
			-"- VS Powell (13th London Regt att) } 15 10/18	
			-"- AD Lacey } 16 10/18	
			2/Lt. CJB James } 16 10/18	
			-"- CC Veitch (7th London Regt att) } 16 10/18	
			Lt. CL Judges MC (2nd Leinster Regt att) } 5 10/18	
			2/Lt. RWA Knox -"- } 5 10/18	
			2/Lt. R Knox -"- } 5 10/18	
			" JP Greene -"- } 5 10/18	
			" A McSparrow -"- } 5 10/18	
			Lt. GC Willoughby 22 10/18	
			Capt HAW Backhoff MM 28 10/18	
			2/Lt ES Powell Cross-posted from 2/10 LR 9 10/18	
			Other ranks:- 124	
			31-10-18	
			A. Grover Lieut Colonel Comdg "The Rangers" 12th London Regt	

(A7092). Wt. W12839/M1293. 750,000. 1/17. D. D. & L., Ltd. Forms/C.2118/14.

14

175/5-8 Army Form C. 2118.

12 London Regt

WO 23

WAR DIARY
or
INTELLIGENCE SUMMARY.
(Erase heading not required.)

Instructions regarding War Diaries and Intelligence Summaries are contained in F. S. Regs., Part II. and the Staff Manual respectively. Title pages will be prepared in manuscript.

Place	Date	Hour	Summary of Events and Information	Remarks and references to Appendices
AIX	1/11/18		Battalion training - Range practice + PT + BF.	
	2nd		Battalion marched to RUMEGIES for Ceremonial Parade by Brigadier General - Ground I.7.B. Afternoon spent in recreation + games -	
	3rd		Battalion Church Parade.	
	4,5+6th		Battalion training - Range practice, PT+BF, Specialist training - Afternoons - Recreation + games	
	6th		Warning order received for Battalion to be prepared to move at 24 hours notice from 1200 hrs today.	
	6th 7th		Battalion training etc.	
QUESNOY	8th		Battalion moved to QUESNOY by march route into Divisional Reserve - Remained night in Billets -	
	9th		Advance was continued at 1000 hrs - Battalion forming part of main body - Crossed canal at MAULDE in general direction for PERUWELZ. - 9TH LONDON REGT forming Advance Guard -	
PERUWELZ			Arrived PERUWELZ at 1800 hours + remained night in billets - 9th LONDON REGT formed outpost line on EAST side of ETOING Canal -	
	10th		Battalion was detailed to form Advance Guard for Brigade and passed through outpost line at 0730 hours and advanced through BASECLES, QUEVAUCAMPS, STAMBRUGES and crossed Canal continuing advance to NEUFMAISON. No opposition encountered. - Civilians co-operated in bridging canals, filling in mine craters etc + advance was therefore not held up -	
NEUFMAISON			Remained night in billets + established outpost outside village - 10th LONDON REGT also at this village - 9th LONDON REGT in Brigade Reserve at ESCACHERIES. - Enemy located at HERCHIES	
	11th	11 am	Received wire from 175th Infantry Bde as follows:- "10th + 12th Bns" "BM. 153 - 11th inst" "Hostilities cease 1100 today aaa Troops will stand" "fast on the outpost line already established aaa All military precautions" "will be observed and there will be no communication with the enemy aaa" "Further instructions later aaa Acknowledge" - ends -	
			The news were received calmly -	

(A7092). Wt. W12839/M1293. 750,000. 1/17. D. D. & L., Ltd. Forms/C.2118/14.

Instructions regarding War Diaries and Intelligence Summaries are contained in F. S. Regs., Part II. and the Staff Manual respectively. Title pages will be prepared in manuscript.

WAR DIARY
or
INTELLIGENCE SUMMARY.
(Erase heading not required.)

Army Form C. 2118.

Place	Date	Hour	Summary of Events and Information	Remarks and references to Appendices
NEUF MAISON	12/11/18		Battalion resting –	
	13th		Battalion moved back into Billets at STAMBRUGES & were very comfortable –	
	14th		A Brigade Service of Thanksgiving was held at 1030 hrs today upon conclusion of Armistice – Massed bands of 10th + 12th LONDON REGTS in attendance –	
			Recreation in afternoon –	
	15th + 16th		Battalion training – P.T., Musketry, Battalion drill &c	
	[illegible]		Recreation in afternoon –	
	17th		Church Parade at Theatre 0945 hours – Roman Catholic Civic procession held in village & 12th Bn Band in attendance also party sent from Battalion to take part in procession –	
	18th		Brigade Ceremonial Parade at A.30.d.5.2 – Massed bands of 9th, 10th + 12th Battalions in attendance.	
	19 + 20th		Battalion training – Recreation in afternoon – Concerts arranged for evenings in Theatre	
	21st		Brigade Ceremonial Parade at 1000 hrs. – Recreation in afternoon	
	22nd		Battalion route march	
	23		Training	
	24th		Church Parade in Theatre at 11.15 hours.	
	25th		Battalion training in P.T – Cross country runs –	
	26th		ditto – P.T, Musketry, L.G, Bn Ceremonial parade &c	
			Recreations + educational classes in afternoon –	
	28th		Battalion route march –	
			Afternoon devoted to education classes + Recreation	
	29th		Training in billets in Musketry, LG &c after Coys bathed –	
			Recreation + education classes in afternoon.	
	30		Battalion parade for practice Inspection – in view of Army Commanders' Inspection	
			Recreation + education classes in afternoon –	

(A7092). Wt. W12839/M1293. 750,000. 1/17. D. D. & L., Ltd. Forms/C.2118/14.

Army Form C. 2118.

Instructions regarding War Diaries and Intelligence Summaries are contained in F. S. Regs., Part II. and the Staff Manual respectively. Title pages will be prepared in manuscript.

WAR DIARY
or
INTELLIGENCE SUMMARY.
(Erase heading not required.)

Place	Date	Hour	Summary of Events and Information	Remarks and references to Appendices
			Casualties for month of November:-	
			Officers :- Killed, Wounded + Missing NIL.	
			Other Ranks :- Killed, NIL – Died of Wounds NIL, Wounded NIL, Missing NIL	
			Reinforcements for month :-	
			Capt H.A.W. Backhoff joined 28/10/18	
			Lieut E.C. Wallace } " B.S. Compton } –"– 4/11/18 from VI Corps Sch.	
			" C.P. Pearse –"– 15/11/18	
			" A.J. Reincke –"– 18/11/18	
			2/Lt J. Horsfield } 2/Lt S.J. Lambourne } –"– 21/11/18	
			+ 81 ors.	
			A. Grover Lieut Colonel Comdg. "The Rangers" 12th London Regt.	
			30-11-18	

(A7092). Wt. W12839/M1293. 750,000. 1/17. D. D. & L., Ltd. Forms/C.2118/14

6

Instructions regarding War Diaries and Intelligence Summaries are contained in F. S. Regs., Part II. and the Staff Manual respectively. Title pages will be prepared in manuscript.

WAR DIARY
or
INTELLIGENCE SUMMARY.
(Erase heading not required.)

Army Form C. 2118.

12 London Rgt

Vol 24

Place	Date	Hour	Summary of Events and Information	Remarks and references to Appendices
STAMBRUGES.	1-12-18		Church Parade held in Theatre at 1030 hrs - Afternoon devoted to recreation -	
	2-12-18		Battalion marched to Aviation Ground, GLANDGLISE for inspection by G.O.C 1st ARMY	
	3rd		Battalion training - P.T+B.F, - NCO instruction under RSM - Musketry, L.G., Ceremonial parade - Specialist training. Afternoon devoted to recreation + educational classes. Two Coys, Transport + QM personnel at Baths.	
	4th		Battalion route march for today, cancelled, owing to inclement weather - Training carried on in billets.	
	5th		Visit by H.M. The KING, - Battalion grouped up at 1130 hrs. - Training in P.T. + Guard duties -	
	6th		Route march - route BELOEIL, St ANNE, QUEVAUCAMPS, STAMBRUGES	
	7th		Battalion training - afternoon devoted to classes + recreation -	
	8th		Church Parade - Theatre at 1115 hours - Afternoon - sport + studies -	
	9th		Training in Guard duties, handling of arms, platoon drill &c	
	10		Battalion bathing - afterwards, training as yesterday -	
	11th & 12th		Training, including PT, Squad drill, Musketry, Ceremonial duties + Ceremonial Guard mounting -	
	13th		Battalion cross-country run - Recreation in afternoon	
	14th		Battalion training - Afternoon devoted to recreation -	
	15th		Church Parade	
	16th		Training - PT + B.F, Squad drill, Musketry, Ceremonial Guard mounting, Specialist training -	
	17th		Battalion bathing -	
	18th		Battalion attended Brigade Parade at 1000 hrs - Afternoon devoted to recreation &c	
	19		Training in billets owing to inclement weather -	
	20		Battalion moved to billets at LEUZE. Parade 0900 hours - Arrived LEUZE at 1230 hours - Billets were found to be very good -	
	21st		Improvement of billets &c - afternoon devoted to recreation -	

(A7092). Wt. W12839/M1293. 750,000. 1/17. D. D. & L., Ltd. Forms/C.2118/14.

Instructions regarding War Diaries and Intelligence Summaries are contained in F. S. Regs., Part II. and the Staff Manual respectively. Title pages will be prepared in manuscript.

WAR DIARY
or
INTELLIGENCE SUMMARY.
(Erase heading not required.)

Army Form C. 2118.

Place	Date	Hour	Summary of Events and Information	Remarks and references to Appendices
LEUZE	22-12-18		Church Parade in Cinema, Rue St Martin –	
	23rd		Battalion training until 1100 hrs – remainder of day devoted to making arrangements for Xmas festivities & recreation –	
	24th		Battalion bathed at Baths in the village	
	25th		Church Parade for Xmas Day Services – Xmas dinners commenced at 12 noon, the Commanding Officer visiting each Company in turn –	
	26th		Companies at disposal of Coy Commanders.	
	27th		Parades cancelled owing to inclement weather –	
	28th		Cleaning up of billets inspection by Commanding Officer	
	29th		Church Parade	
	30th		Battalion training – Boxing &c. Few men bathed – Afternoon devoted to recreation &c	
	31st		Battalion training – Boxing &c Afternoon devoted to recreation &c.	

"THE RANGERS" 12th LONDON REGT. ORDERLY ROOM No. .... Date ....

[illegible] .... LT. COLONEL.
COMDG. "THE RANGERS" 12th LONDON REGT.

(A7092). Wt. W12839/M1293. 750,000. 1/17. D. D. & L., Ltd. Forms/C.2118/14.

58

Army Form C. 2118.

12 London Regt

Vol 27

WAR DIARY
or
INTELLIGENCE SUMMARY.

(Erase heading not required.)

Instructions regarding War Diaries and Intelligence Summaries are contained in F. S. Regs., Part II. and the Staff Manual respectively. Title pages will be prepared in manuscript.

Place	Date	Hour	Summary of Events and Information	Remarks and references to Appendices
LEUZE BELGIUM.	1st JAN/19		Battalion training including Guard duties, P.T. + musketry. Boxing. Afternoon devoted to sport &c	
	2nd		-do- -do- -do-	
	3rd		Battalion bathing - training carried out afterwards -	
	4th		Battalion training including Guard duties &c &c	
	5th		Church Parade	
	6th to 10th		Battalion training including Guard duties, PT + musketry, Boxing - Afternoon devoted to sport &c	
	11th		Interior Economy - Inspection of billets by Commanding Officer -	
	12th		Church Parade	
	13th 14 + 15th		Battalion training + boxing - afternoon devoted to sport &c	
	16th		Battalion bathing - training afterwards -	
	17th		Training in P.T. Guard duties, platoon + Battalion Ceremonial drill -	
	18th		Cleaning up + inspection of billets -	
	19th		Church Parade.	
	20 - 24th		Battalion training + boxing - Afternoon devoted to Sport.	
	25th		Cleaning up + Inspection of Billets by G.O.C. Brigade + the Commanding Officer	
	26th		Church Parade	
	27 + 28th		Training and boxing &c. under Company arrangements	
	29 + 30th		Owing to fall of snow, Companies arranged route marches independently -	
	31st		Training under Company arrangements -	

[signature] Lt. Colonel
Comdg. "The Rangers," 12th London Regt.

6   12 London Regt   58

Army Form C. 2118.

Instructions regarding War Diaries and Intelligence Summaries are contained in F. S. Regs., Part II. and the Staff Manual respectively. Title pages will be prepared in manuscript.

WAR DIARY or INTELLIGENCE SUMMARY.

(Erase heading not required.)

96

Place	Date	Hour	Summary of Events and Information	Remarks and references to Appendices
LEUZE BELGIUM	FEBY 1919		Demobilisation figures for JANUARY 1919 :- Major J P CRITCHLEY (1/4 KOYLI); LIEUT A D LACEY; CAPT A SHEPHERD (9th LON R) (Demobion leave); LIEUT L. DUCKETT MC; 2/LT CJB JAMES; Lt+QM H BLENKINSOP; LIEUT V S POWELL (13th LON R)	122 other ranks
	1st		Battalion bathing -	
	2nd		Church Parade -	
	3rd		Training - boxing. Company lectures upon conditions of the Army of Occupation &c.	
	4th		Training + bathing -	
	5th		Training + bathing - afternoons devoted to sport	
	6th		Interior economy - Inspection of billets	
	7 + 8th		Training + boxing &c	
	8th		Draft of 8 Officers + 120 other ranks left LEUZE to join 2/16th LONDON REGT at CALAIS for Army of Occupation	
	9th		Church Parade - Amalgamation of "A"+"C" and "B"+"D" Companies -	
	10th		Interior economy - closing in of billets owing to drafts + demobilized men leaving Companies -	
	11th		Companies at Coy Commander's disposal	
	12th		Battalion bathed -	
	13th + 14th		Companies at disposal of Coy Commanders.	
	15th		Interior economy - amalgamation of Companies under command of Lt (A/Capt) L. B. BELL	
	16th		Church Parade -	
	17th		Interior economy - closing up of billets + centralisation	
	18th + 19th		Composite Coy at disposal of O.C. Coy	
	20th		Bn bathing - Draft of 67 ors (of total of 90) proceeded to join 9th London Regt for Army of Occupation	
	21st + 22nd		Interior economy. Coy at disposal of Company commander -	

(A7092). Wt. W12839/M1293. 750,000. 1/17. D. D. & L., Ltd. Forms/C.2118/14.

Army Form C. 2118.

WAR DIARY
or
INTELLIGENCE SUMMARY.
(Erase heading not required.)

Instructions regarding War Diaries and Intelligence Summaries are contained in F. S. Regs., Part II. and the Staff Manual respectively. Title pages will be prepared in manuscript.

Place	Date	Hour	Summary of Events and Information	Remarks and references to Appendices
LEUZE	23rd Feby 1919		Church Parade	
	24th + 25th		Interior economy – Coy at disposal of Coy Commander	
	26th to 28th		– ditto – – ditto –	
			Officers + o.r. demobilised during month as under:-	

1-2-19	Lieut C.R PEARSE	35 ors.
7-2-19	" A S COMPTON	46
8-2-19	" H.D. PEABODY DCM	3
9-2-19	CAPT SAS MALKIN (RAMC)	-
10-2-19	–	20
13-2-19	–	13
14-2-19	–	16
21-2-19	CAPT A E ELLIS.	-
15-2-19	–	18
16-2-19	–	13
17-2-19	–	32
14-2-19	2/Lt RE MALLISON.	–
20-2-19	–	28
23-2-19	–	1
28-2-19	Lt FC WALLACE	11

"THE RANGERS" ORDERLY ROOM No. R/........ Date........ 12th LONDON REGT.

A Crosse ....LT.-COLONEL.
COMDG. "THE RANGERS," 12th LONDON REGT.

(A7092). Wt. W12839/M1293 750,000. 1/17. D. D. & L., Ltd. Forms/C.2118/14.

Army Form C. 2118.

WAR DIARY
or
INTELLIGENCE SUMMARY.
(Erase heading not required.)

Instructions regarding War Diaries and Intelligence Summaries are contained in F. S. Regs., Part II. and the Staff Manual respectively. Title pages will be prepared in manuscript.

Vol 28

Place	Date	Hour	Summary of Events and Information	Remarks and references to Appendices
LEUZE	1·3·19		Church Parade	
	2·3·19		Interior Economy Coy at disposal of Coy Commander.	
	3·3·19		— Ditto — — Ditto —	
	4·3·19		— ditto — — ditto —	
	5·3·19		— " — — " —	
	6·3·19		— " — — " —	
	7·3·19		— " —	
	8·3·19		Inspection of billets	
	9·3·19		Church Parade	
	10·3·19		Interior Economy — " —	
	11·3·19		— " —	
	12·3·19		— " — — " — — " —	
	13·3·19		— " — — " — — " —	
	14·3·19		— " — — " — — " — — " — Muster Parade 0830 hours.	
	15·3·19		— " — — " — — " — — " — 1345 "	
	16·3·19		Church Parade.	
	17·3·19		Interior Economy Coy at the disposal of Coy Commander.	
	18·3·19		— " — — " —	
	19·3·19		Baths.	
	20·3·19		Interior Economy — " —	
	21·3·19		— " —	
	22·3·19	1000hrs	Inspection of Billets by C.O.	
	23·3·19	1030 "	Church Parade.	
	24·3·19		Interior Economy. Coy at disposal of O.C. Coy.	
	25·3·19		— " — — " — — " —	
	26·3·19		— " —	
	27·3·19		Kit Inspection by O.C. Coy.	
	28·3·19		Baths.	
	29·3·19		Interior Economy. Coy at O.C. Coy's disposal	
	30·3·19		Church Parade	
	31·3·19		Interior Economy Coy at — " —	

Demobilization figures for March.

Major [illegible] Wyatt.
Capt. S.C. Mann.
Lt. G.C. Willoughby
Lt. E.R. Gunton
2/Lt. J.S. [illegible] Hetherington.
2/Lt. R.B.H. Rigby
2/Lt. J.G. Tally — 29 O.Rs.

9th London Offrs. Demobilized March

Capt. J. Maggson.
Lieut. R.G. Bagshaff. M.C.
2/Lt. L. Stephens
2/Lt. W.L. Bagnal.
2/Lt. P.W. Wills M.C.
2/Lt. J.L.R. Davies
Lieut. G.F. Fletcher

H.W. Wackett Capt.
for LT.-COLONEL,
COMDG. "THE RANGERS," 12th LONDON REGT.

"THE RANGERS" ORDERLY ROOM No. R/...... Date...... 12th LONDON REGT.

(A7092) Wt. W12839/M1293 750,000. 1/17. D. D. & L., Ltd. Forms/C2118/14.

APRIL 1919
MISSING

Instructions regarding War Diaries and Intelligence Summaries are contained in F. S. Regs., Part II. and the Staff Manual respectively. Title pages will be prepared in manuscript.

WAR DIARY
or
INTELLIGENCE SUMMARY.

(*Erase heading not required.*)

Army Form C. 2118.

12 London Regt

Vol 29

Place	Date	Hour	Summary of Events and Information	Remarks and references to Appendices
Louze.	1/5/19		Bathe from 1400 hrs. to 1600 hrs.	
	2/5/19		Company at disposal of O.C. Coy. Rifle inspection	
	3/5/19		— —	
	4/5/19	1030	Church Parade	
	5/5/19		Company at disposal of O.C. Coy.	
	6/5/19		— — "	
	7/5/19		— —	
	8/5/19		— — "	
	9/5/19		— —	
	10/5/19		— Rifle inspection	
	11/5/19		Church Parade	
	12/5/19		Company at disposal of O.C. Coy.	
	13/5/19		—	
	14/5/19		— —	
	15/5/19		— —	
	16/5/19		— —	
	17/5/19		—	
	18/5/19	1030hrs	Church Parade	
	19/5/19		Coy at disposal of O.C. Coy.	
	20/5/19		—	
	21/5/19		—	
	22/5/19		—	
	23/5/19		—	
	24/5/19		—	
	25/5/19		Church Parade	
	26/5/19		Coy at disposal of O.C. Coy.	
	27/5/19		— —	
	28/5/19		— " —	
	29/5/19		— —	
	30/5/19		— " — F.M.O. Inspection	
	31/5/19		—	

"THE RANGERS" ORDERLY ROOM No. .... Date .... 12th LONDON REGT.

A. Groves
..............................LT.-COLONEL,
COMDG. "THE RANGERS," 12th LONDON REGT.

(A7092). Wt. W12839/M1293. 750,000. 1/17. D. D. & L., Ltd. Forms/C.2118/14.

www.ingramcontent.com/pod-product-compliance
Lightning Source LLC
Chambersburg PA
CBHW081427160426
43193CB00013B/2209